The Joy of Sex

A Cordon Bleu Guide to Lovemaking

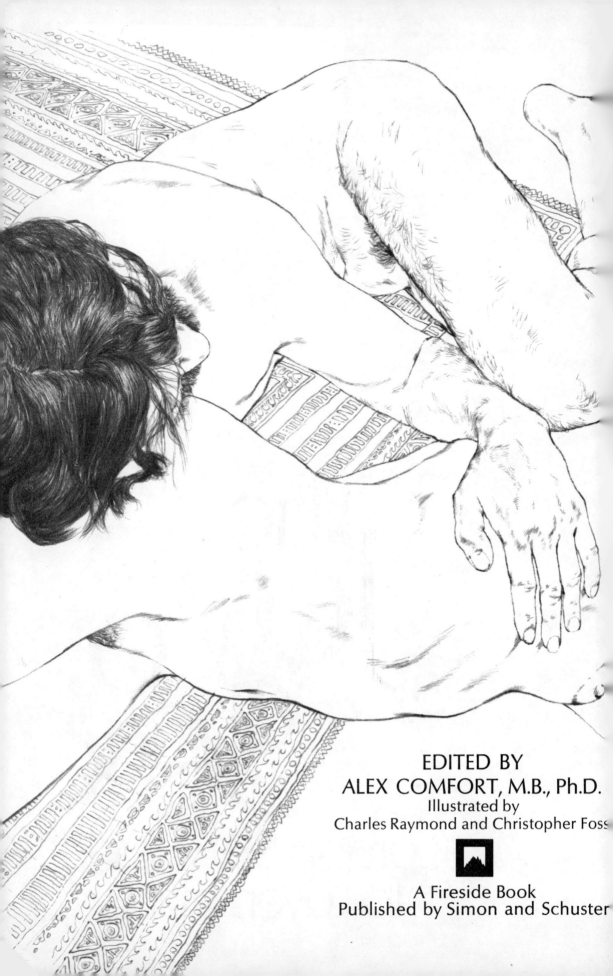

EDITED BY
ALEX COMFORT, M.B., Ph.D.
Illustrated by
Charles Raymond and Christopher Foss

A Fireside Book
Published by Simon and Schuster

The Joy of Sex

A Cordon Bleu Guide
to Lovemaking

Contents

General Editor: Alex Comfort
House Editor: Max Monsarrat
Designer: Janette Palmer

Art Director: Peter Kindersley

The publishers would like to
thank the artists, Charles
Raymond and Christopher
Foss, for the care and
devotion they have lavished
on their illustrations for
The Joy of Sex. They have
throughout worked closely
with the Editor to reflect the
style of this book – its
humour, honesty and
directness. The results are a
magnificent tribute to their
skill and dedication.

Sauces & Pickles 149

Problems 223

Preface

A biologist-writer interested in human sexual behavior is asked to read many prospective books – admonitary, weird, religious, naive, conventional or just plain ignorant – all of them aiming to be helpful, and none of them getting the key quite right.

This book is based originally on the work of one couple. One of them is a practicing physician; their anonymity is accordingly professional, and the final text incorporates the suggestions of several couples, plus a few experts. The basic idea struck me as unique. A cookery book is a sophisticated and unanxious account of available dishes – culinary fantasies as well as staple diets – with the practical details provided. This book is an equally unanxious account of the full repertoire of human hetero-sexuality. As such, it is long overdue. A cookbook tells the novice how to tackle a live lobster, what to do when the mayonnaise separates, how to fix a chateaubriand. The authors of this book describe, in the same unruffled detail, and with a sense of fun, what to do about impotence or premature ejaculation, how to manage oral sex, how to play symbolically aggressive games, how to treat a partner who is hip for 'discipline,' how not to be bothered by fetishes, how to use kinky clothes as sex stimuli. A good many professional counselors react to such questions – when clients have the pluck to ask them – if not with psychiatric and moral anxiety, at least with a lack of detailed knowhow. Doctors can't necessarily know your needs from their own sex lives, and not all of them have much idea of the range and variety of human sexual behaviors: I wish I had read such a recipe book as a medical student.

I have done little to the original draft apart from expansion to cover more topics: the authors' choice of emphases and their light-hearted style have been left alone. Where explanation is needed (and explanation, in conventionally anxious matters, helps) they introduce depth-psychology in a jargonless form. This is the right approach at a moment when primatology and classical human psychodynamics look like joining hands, and for some of the explanatory biology I am to blame.

It is difficult to produce anything really new in the field of 'sex education.' The permissive society has permitted everything from worried and po-faced admonition to eccentric porn. Most book-stalls carry a rash of 'straight' books which stop short of answers, and 'counseling' magazines based on unpractical, if not pathological, fantasy. It is high time adult readers were treated to some humane and experienced sense. I hope that the book will prove as useful to professional counselors as to couples, but it is the ordinary, sexually active, reader – anxious both to enjoy sexuality and to be responsible about it – who should benefit most.

Alex Comfort

On Advanced Lovemaking

All of us who are not disabled or dumb are able to dance and sing—after a fashion. This, if you think about it, summarizes the justification for learning to make love. Love, like singing, is something to be taken spontaneously. On the other hand, the difference between Pavlova and the Palais de Danse, or opera and barber-shop singing, is much less than the difference between sex as the last generation came to accept it and sex as it can be.

At least we recognize this now (so that instead of worrying if sex is sinful, most people now worry whether they are 'getting satisfaction'—one can worry about anything, given the determination). There are now enough books about the basics: the main use of these is to get rid of worries over the normality, possibility, and variety of sexual experience. The people who go to Masters and Johnson are getting over hangups so basic that in past generations the folk tradition would have taken care of them. At least the 'permissive' scene in publishing removed some of this cover-up. Our book is slightly different, in that there are now enough people who have the basics and really need hard information (not simply reassurance).

Chef-grade cooking doesn't happen naturally: it starts at the point where people know how to prepare and enjoy food, are curious about it and willing to take trouble preparing it, read recipe hints, and find they are helped by one or two detailed techniques. It's hard to make mayonnaise by trial and error, for instance. Cordon Bleu sex, as we define it, is exactly the same situation—the extra one can get from comparing notes, using some imagination, trying way-out or new experiences, when one already is making satisfying love and wants to go on from there.

It is always sad when a love relationship runs aground through non-communication (fear of rejection over some fantasy need, inability to come to terms with aggressive needs through a misplaced idea of tenderness, inability to accept sexuality as play). These hangups, plus monotony, are a large part of all five- or seven-year itches, and, between loving and tolerant people, avoidable.

We shall have four sorts of readers; those who don't fancy it, find it disturbing and would rather stay the way they are, with Reuben sandwiches—these should put it down, accept our apologies, and stay the way they are: those who are with the idea, but don't like our choice of techniques—these should remember it's a menu, not a rulebook. We have tried to stay wide-open, but it is always difficult to write about things one doesn't enjoy, and we have left out long discussion of the very specialized—one-legged ladies, mackintoshes—and things like S and M, which aren't really love or even sex in quite our sense of the word. People who like these know already what they want to try. One aim of this book is to cure the notion, born of non-discussion, that common sex needs are odd or weird. As to the general repertoire, the whole joy of sex-with-love is that there are no rules, so long as you enjoy, and the choice is practically unlimited. This is the way most people will use our notes—as a personal one-couple notebook from which they might get ideas. Then there are the hardy experimentalists, bent on trying absolutely everything· They too will do best to read this exactly like a cookbook—except that sex is safer in this respect, between lovers, in that you can't get obese or atherosclerotic on it, or give yourself ulcers. The worst you can get is sore, anxious or disappointed. Sex must be physically the safest of all human activities (leaving out social repercussions). You can have infinite variety to taste. But one needs a steady basic diet of quiet, night-and-morning matrimonial intercourse to stand this experimentation on, simply because, contrary to popular ideas, the more regular sex a couple has the higher the deliberately contrived peaks—just as the more you cook routinely, the better and the more reliable banquets you can stage.

Finally, the people we are addressing are the adventurous and uninhibited lovers who want to find the limits of their ability to enjoy sex. That means we take some things for granted—having intercourse naked and spending time over it; being able and willing to make it last, up to a whole afternoon on occasion; having privacy and washing facilities; not being scared of things like genital kisses; not being obsessed with one sexual trick to the exclusion of all others, and, of course, loving each other.

This book is about love as well as sex as the title implies: you don't get high-quality sex on any other basis—either you love each other before you come to want it, or, if you happen to get it, you love each other because of it, or both. No point in arguing this, but just as you can't cook without heat you can't make love without feedback (which may be the reason we say 'make love' rather than 'make sex'). Sex is the one place where we today can learn to treat people as people. Feedback means the right mixture of stop and go, tough and tender, exertion and affection. This comes by empathy and long mutual knowledge. Anyone who *expects* to get this in a first attempt with a stranger is an optimist, or a neurotic—if he does, it is what used to be called love at first sight, and isn't expendable: 'skill', or variety, is no substitute. Also one can't teach tenderness.

This is a book about valid sexual behaviors, plus a certain amount about how and why they work. It isn't a dictionary: in particular we've avoided a lot of the name-entries attached to particular sorts of performance at the start of the century—the reason is that they are largely out of date. Rather than sticking on labels like narcissism or sadomasochism, biologists and psychiatrists now tend to start by looking at actual behaviors and seeing what use they are or what they signify. Lump names are a handy shorthand, but they tend to be offputting, especially when very general human behaviors get a label which makes them sound like an illness; and they tend to trigger pointless collectors'-piece arguments, for example whether 'women are naturally masochistic' because they get penetrated rather than doing the penetrating.

We haven't started with a short lecture on the biology and psychology of human sex: instead we've put a little about it into the various entries. Most people now know that man's 'sexuality' starts at birth and runs continuously from mother-child to man-woman relations, that it involves some periods of programmed anxiety about the genitals ('castration fears') which probably served originally to stop young apes from falling foul of their fathers, but which, in man, are building stones for a lot of other adult behaviors; and that the wide range of human sex needs of all kinds controlled by this unique developmental background—long childhood, close mother-child contact but a taboo on mother-child or father-child sex, close pair-bonding which centers in sexual play, the way bird pair-formation centers in nest-building and display (this is the phenomenon more often described as love), and so on. Without going into details we've mentioned throughout the book how parts of this human background fit into the pattern of what humans enjoy sexually. Most human sex behaviors 'mean' a whole range of different things (the in-word is that they are 'overdetermined' —for examples of what this means in practice see what we've written about *Clothes,* for instance).

A little theory makes sex more interesting, more comprehensible, and less scarey—too much is a put-down, especially as you're likely to get it out of perspective and become a spectator of your own performance. If you have really troublesome hangups you need an expert to hold the mirror for you and go personally into what they mean— self-adhesive labels are actively unhelpful. All humans are sadistic, narcissistic, masochistic, bisexual and what have you—if you stuck on all the labels you would look like a cabin trunk. What matters is whether any of the behaviors in which you engage are bothering you or other people—if so, they are a useful pointer to what the problem is, but no more than that.

The starting point of all lovemaking is close bodily contact. Love has been defined as the harmony of two souls and the contact of two epidermes. It is also, from our infancy, the starting point of human relationships and needs. Our culture ('Anglo-Saxon'), after several centuries of intense taboos on many such contacts—between friends, between males—which are used by other cultures, has cut down 'intimacy' based on bodily contact to parent-child and lover-lover situations. We're getting over this taboo, or at least the part which has spilled over into baby-raising and explicit lovemaking, but coupled with our other cultural reservation, which says that play and fantasy are only safe for children, it has dealt us a bad hand for really full and personal sex. Our idea of sex wouldn't be recognizable to some other cultures, though our range of choice is the widest ever. For a start it's over-genital: 'sex' for our culture means putting the penis in the vagina. Man's whole skin is a genital organ. As to touching, proximity and so on, see Desmond Morris's brilliant account in *Intimate Behavior,* which catalogues our hangups. Good sex is about the only adult remedy for these.

There isn't too much point in crying over cultural spilt milk. *Our sex repertoire has to be geared to us as we are, not to Trobriand Islanders (who have their own different hangups). We need extensive sex play which is centered in intercourse and in doing things.* At the same time we might as well plan our menu so that we learn to use the rest of our equipment. That includes our whole skin surface, our feelings of identity, aggression and so on, and all of our fantasy needs. Luckily, sex behavior in humans is enormously elastic (it has had to be, or we wouldn't be here), and also nicely geared to help us express most of the needs which society or our upbringing have corked up. Elaboration in sex is something we need rather specially (though it isn't confined to our sort of society) and it has the advantage that if we really make it work it makes us more, not less, receptive to each other as people. This is the answer to anyone who thinks that conscious effort to increase our sex range is 'mechanical' or a substitute for treating each other as people—we may start that way, but it's an excellent entry to learning that we are people—probably the only one our sort of society can really use at the moment. There may be other places we can learn to express all of ourselves, and do it mutually, but there aren't many.

Those are our assumptions. Granted this feedback and mutual exploration, there are two modes of sex, the duet and the solo, and a good concert alternates between them. The duet is a cooperative effort aiming at simultaneous orgasm, or at least one orgasm each, and complete, untechnically planned let-go. This in fact needs skill, and can be built up from more calculated 'love-play' until doing the right thing for both of you becomes fully automatic. This is the basic sexual meal. The solo, by contrast, is when one partner is the player and the other the instrument; the aim of the player is to produce results on the other's pleasure experience as extensive, unexpected and generally wild as his or her skill allows—to blow them out of themselves. The player doesn't lose control, though he or she can get wildly excited by what is happening to the other. The instrument *does* lose control—in fact, with a responsive instrument and a skillful performer, this is the concerto situation—if it ends in an uncontrollable ensemble, so much the better. All the elements of music and the dance get into this scene —rhythm, mounting tension, tantalization, even actual aggression: 'I'm like the executioner,' said the lady in the Persian poem, 'but where he inflicts intolerable pain I will only make you die of pleasure.' There is indeed an element of aggression or infliction in the solo mode, which is why some lovers dislike it and others overdo it, but no major lovemaking is complete without some solo passages.

The antique idea of the woman as passive and the man as performer used to ensure that he would show off playing solos on her, and some marriage manuals perpetuate this idea. In a more liberated scene she is herself the soloist par excellence, whether in getting him excited to start with, or in controlling him and showing off all her skills. In fact there is only one really unmusical situation, and that is the reverse of a real solo, where one uses the other to obtain satisfaction, without any attempt at mutuality. True, one may say, 'Do it yourself this time,' as a quick finish, but it is no more than that.

In the old world extended solo techniques have never quite died as a male skill: in Europe at one time calculated solo skill among women was supposed to be limited to prostitutes (most of whom conspicuously lack it, for lack of empathy). Now it is on the way back, starting half-heartedly with 'petting to climax,' but getting today to be a polite accomplishment: we shall probably have extension courses soon. This, as usual, will likely go too far, and become a substitute for full, let-go intercourse—whereas in fact it's a preparation, supplement, overture, bridging operation, tailpiece, interlude. The solo-given orgasm is unique, however—neither bigger nor smaller in either sex than in a full duet, but different. We've heard both sexes call it 'sharper but not so round,' and most people who have experienced both like to alternate them; it is also quite different from self-stimulation, which most people like occasionally too. Trying to say how they differ is a little like describing wines. Differ they do, however, and much depends on cultivating and alternating them.

Solo devices are not, of course, necessarily separate from intercourse. Apart from leading into it there are many coital solos—for the woman astride, for example—while mutual masturbation or genital kisses can be fully fledged duets. Nor is it anything to do with 'clitoral' versus 'vaginal' orgasm (this is only a crass anatomical way of trying to verbalize a real difference), since the man feels the same distinction, and you can get a roaring solo orgasm from the skin of the fingertips, the breasts, the soles of the feet, or the earlobes of a receptive woman (less commonly extra-genitally in the man). Coition which ought to be mutual but gives a solo feeling (to her) is what people who talk about 'clitoral orgasm' are trying as a rule to verbalize. Solo-response can be electrifyingly extreme in the quietest people. Skillfully handled by someone who doesn't stop for yells of murder, but does know when to stop, a woman can get orgasm after orgasm, and a man can be kept hanging just short of climax to the limit of human endurance.

Toplevel enjoyment doesn't *have* to be varied, it just often is. In fact, being stuck rigidly with one sex technique usually means anxiety. In this book we have not, for example, gone heavily on things like coital postures. The non-freak ones are now familiar to most people from writing and pictures if not from trial—the freak ones, as a rule, one could think of spontaneously, but few of them have marked advantages except as a spectator sport. Moreover, the technique of straight intercourse, which needs a suspension of self-observation, doesn't lend itself to treatment in writing, except for elementary students. This explains the apparent emphasis in our book on extras—the sauces and pickles. Most of these are psychologically and biologically geared to cover specific human needs, often left over from a 'civilized' childhood. Individuals who, through a knot in their psyche, are obliged to *live* on sauce and pickle only are unfortunate in missing the most sustaining part of the meal—kinks and exclusive obsessions in sex are very like living exclusively on horseradish sauce through allergy to beef; fear of horseradish sauce as indigestible, unnecessary and immature is another hangup, namely puritanism. As to our choice of needs and/or problems, we've based it on a good many years of listening to people.

In writing descriptively about sex it is hard not to be solemn, however unsolemnly we play in bed. In fact, one of the things still missing from the 'new sexual freedom' is the unashamed ability to use sex as play—in this, psychoanalytic ideas of maturity are nearly as much to blame as oldstyle moralisms about what is normal or perverse. We are all immature, and have anxieties and aggressions. Coital play, like dreaming, is probably man's programmed way of dealing acceptably with these, just as children express their fears and aggressions in games. If they play at Indian tortures, out of jealously of their little brother or the opposite sex, we don't call that sadism: adults are unfortunately afraid of playing games, of dressing up, of acting scenes. It makes them self-conscious: something horrid might get out.

Bed is the place to play all the games you have ever wanted to play, at the play-level—if adults could become less self-conscious about such 'immature' needs we should have fewer deeply anxious and committed fetishists creating a sense of community to enable them to do their thing without feeling isolated. We heard of a frogman who used to make his wife sleep in rubber bedsheets; he had to become a frogman for real, because dressing in a diving-suit for kicks was embarrassing and made him look odd. If we were able to transmit the sense of play which is essential to a full, enterprising and healthily immature view of sex between committed people, we would be performing a mitzvah: people who play flagellation games and are excited by them bother nobody, provided they don't turn off a partner who finds the scenario frightening. People who enact similar aggressions outside the bedroom are apt to end up at My Lai or Belsen. The aim of this book is pleasure, not psychiatry, but we suspect that the two coincide. Play is one function of sexual elaboration—playfulness is a part of love which could well be the major contribution of the Aquarian revolution to human happiness. Hence the association with pregenital and immature sauces and pickles.

But still the main dish is loving, unself-conscious intercourse—long, frequent, varied, ending with both parties satisfied but not so full they can't face another light course, and another meal in a few hours. The *pièce de résistance* is the good old face-to-face matrimonial, the finishing-off position, with mutual orgasm, and starting with a full day or night of ordinary tenderness. Other ways of making love are special in various ways, and the changes of timbre are infinitely varied—complicated ones are for special occasions, or special uses like holding off an over-quick male orgasm, or are things which, like pepper steak, are stunning once a year but not dietary.

If you don't like our repertoire or if it doesn't square with yours, never mind. The aim of *The Joy of Sex* is to stimulate your creative imagination. You can preface your own ideas with 'this is how we play it,' and play it your way. But by that time, when you have tried all your own creative sexual fantasies, you won't need books. Sex books can only suggest techniques to encourage you to experiment.

There are after all only two 'rules' in good sex, apart from the obvious one of not doing things which are silly, antisocial or dangerous. One is 'Don't do anything you don't really enjoy,' and the other is 'Find your partner's needs and don't balk them if you can help it.' In other words, a good giving and taking relationship depends on a compromise (so does going to a show—if you both want the same thing, fine: if not, take turns and don't let one partner always dictate). This can be easier than it sounds, because unless your partner wants something you find actively off-putting, real lovers get a reward not only from their own satisfactions but from seeing the other respond and become satisfied. Most wives who don't like Chinese food will eat it occasionally for the pleasure of seeing a Sinophile husband enjoy it, and vice versa. Partners who won't do this over specific sex needs are usually balking, not because they've tried it and it's a turn-off (many experimental dishes turn out nicer than you expected), but simply through ignorance of the range of human needs, plus being scared if these include things like aggression, cultivating extragenital sensation, or play-acting, which the last half-century's social mythology pretended weren't there. Reading a full list of the unscheduled accessory sex behaviors which some normal people find helpful might be thought a necessary preliminary to any extended sex relationship, particularly marriage if you really intend to stay with it, but so far the books haven't helped much in this respect. If anything they've scared people rather than instructed them.

Couples should match up their needs and preferences (though people don't find these out at once). You won't get to some of our suggestions or understand them until you've learned to respond. It's a mistake to run so long as walking is such an enchanting and new experience, and you may be happy pedestrians who match automatically. Most people who marry rightly prefer to try themselves out and play themselves in. Where a rethink really helps is at the point where you've got used to each other socially (sex needs aren't the only ones which need matching up between people who live together) and feel that the surface needs repolishing. If you think that sexual relations are overrated, it does need repolishing, and you haven't paid enough attention to the wider use of your sexual equipment as a way of communicating totally. The traditional American expedient at the point where the surface gets dull is to trade in the relationship and start all over in an equally uninstructed attempt with someone else, on the offchance of getting a better match-up by random choice. This is emotionally wasteful and you usually repeat the same mistakes. It would be worth trying either to map each other's sex tastes before starting, or to try to learn them if you haven't done so intuitively so far. If you're planting a long term garden it's at least sensible to know a little about the biology of plants. Long-term love expressed in active sex means you have to know something about the biology of people. Don't go in for mutual do-it-yourself psychoanalysis, or you'll bring down the roof on each other. We all have pregenital needs, however we were weaned, potted or reared, just as we all have fingerprints and a navel. Finding out someone else's needs and your own, and how to express them in bed, is not only interesting and educative but rewarding, and what sexual love is about.

Read through or dip into this book together and separately. These are all techniques which some straight people need and use to fill out their sex lives, or simply enjoy as play and relaxation. Don't waste time on things which aren't for you. All the ideas in the book work as a turn-on for some people, virtually none for everyone. Go by your own needs and your partner's. Do note anything which turns one or both of you on to the point of saying 'I'd like to try that.' If you're shy of talking about sexual needs, make a list of the page numbers you'd like your partner to read, and exchange lists (this isn't a plug to make you buy two copies—you can take turns). Then take it mutually from there. You will find out things about each other you didn't know, and all of them will be rewarding.

Colorplates Appearing in Center Insert

The
Art of
Making
Love

'The whole joy of sex-with-love is that there are no rules, so long as you enjoy, and the choice is practically unlimited.'

'You don't get high-quality sex without love and feedback. Feedback means the right mixture of stop and go, tough and tender, exertion and affection.'

'Bed is the right place to play all the games you have ever wanted to play. This is essential to a full, enterprising and healthily immature view of sex between committed people. Take off your shell along with your clothes.'

'There are only two guidelines in good sex, "Don't do anything you don't really enjoy", and "Find out your partner's needs and don't balk them if you can help it."'

'Finding out someone else's needs and your own, and how to express them in bed, is not only interesting and educative, but rewarding, and what sexual love is all about.'

'We must learn to use the whole of our skin surface, our feelings of identity, aggression and so on, and all our fantasy needs.'

'A woman's greatest asset after her beauty is her natural perfume—it comes from the whole of her, hair, skin, breasts, armpits, genitals. The smell and feel of a man's skin probably have more to do with sexual attraction than any other single feature.'

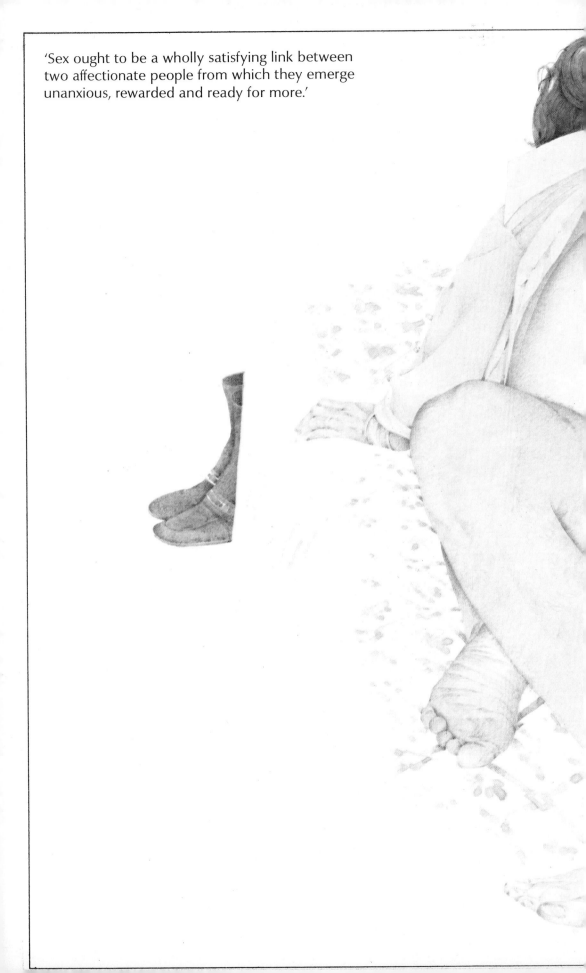

'Sex ought to be a wholly satisfying link between two affectionate people from which they emerge unanxious, rewarded and ready for more.'

'Women who have really learned to enjoy sex are usually fascinated by their partner's penis, as men are by women's breasts, shape, odor and feel, and learn to play with it fully and skillfully. Good hand and mouth work practically guarantee a good partner.'

'Tenderness does not exclude extremely violent games (though many people neither need nor want these) but it is shown fully in the way you touch each other.'

'Women often fail to use enough pressure, especially in handwork, though the light variety is a sensation on its own. Start very gently, making full use of the skin surface and work up. Male strength, on the other hand, is a turn-on in sex, but it isn't expressed in clumsiness, bear hugs and brute force.

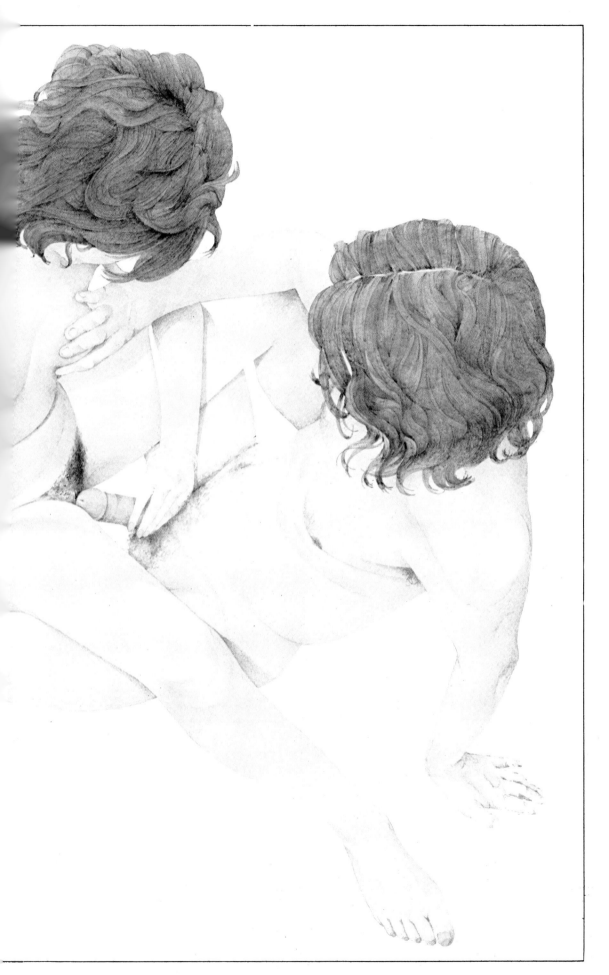

'Male sexual response is far brisker and more automatic than women's: it is triggered by *things*. Your clothes, breasts, odor, etc. aren't what he loves instead of you—simply the things he needs to set sex in motion to express love.'

'Uninhibited partners will tell each other about their fantasies (try free-associating just before orgasm if you are shy). Really communicating partners look for them and put them on the menu unannounced—there is no more complete communication.'

'Women probably differ sexually more than men.
Never assume that you don't need to relearn for
each person.'

'Planning and thinking about sex to come is part of love. So is lying together in complete luxury afterwards.'

'Cordon bleu sex is the extra one can get from comparing notes, using some imagination, trying way-out or new experiences, when one is already making satisfying love and wants to go from there.'

Starters
the basic ingredients

beds

Still the most important piece of domestic sexual equipment. Really enthusiastic sex usually involves at one time or another almost every piece of furniture in the house, at least experimentally, but the bed is its commonest venue. Most beds on the market are designed by people who think they are intended to sleep on. The problem arises from the fact that the ideal surface for most kinds of intercourse needs to be rather harder than is comfortable for a whole night's sleep. One solution is to have two beds, one for sex and the other for sleeping, but this is a counsel of luxury, and in any case the need to move disrupts the best part of the night, the total relaxation which follows complete love.

The best advice is probably to settle for a compromise and have a mattress on the floor as well. Enormous or circular beds look suggestive but have no real advantages over a full-size double bed. There are a few points we would consider before giving a seal of approval. First, since one uses the sides as well as the surface, the height needs to be right. The top of the mattress should be exactly level with the man's pubic bone – then, if you put your partner on or over it, she will be at the right height from in front or from behind. For some operations, especially bondage scenes if you like them, bedposts are essential, preferably tall ones, like those which hold up the canopy of old European beds, but not, for choice, a foot-board, as you may want to use the end edge to start with, moving directly to full-length. Massive old bed-frames have great advantages, in that they don't rattle or collapse. The mattress needs to be as hard as you can tolerate for comfortable sleep. Anything less forfeits the chief sexual joy of living and sleeping together – the fact that you can take one another at any hour of the night when both want it, and relax together immediately afterwards. If you have room, have a single bed as well, in case either partner is sick and feels more comfortable solo – twin beds have no place in a full sexual relationship.

Beside the bed itself you need four pillows – two very hard to go under the buttocks, and two soft, to sleep on. The room must be warm at all times of the year – warm enough to sleep without getting chilled and without bedclothes if you wish. Electric blankets shouldn't therefore be necessary – the sort you lie upon will in any case not stand up to sexual intercourse. Unless you are very prosperous and it excites you to set up a special 'sex room,' bedroom chairs and stools can be chosen without too much ostentation to complete the necessary equipment for all eventualities (see *Equipment*), together with a soft rug, soft enough to be really comfortable for the underneath party, and mirrors. You also need enough bedside drawers to hold extras which you may need on impulse without having to get up and find them – lubricants, contraceptives, vibrators and so on. A well-designed bedroom can be a sexual gymnasium without it being embarrassing to let elderly relatives leave their coats there.

Water-beds are a relative innovation. They can indeed produce extraordinary sensations, and they have a natural period of resonance which tends to take over – one has to move in their rhythm, but this itself is a stimulating constraint. Expensive – best kept for the odd extramural occasion when you re-honeymoon in a hotel room that's fitted with one. With the spread of inflatables we may see a whole range of new sexual furniture-surfaces in the next few years.

birdsong at morning

What your partner says in orgasm should never be quoted at him or her – it can be played back when you are both in a suitable mood, but only then. It is the one time when people are spiritually most naked. There is a striking consistency, over ages and continents, in what women say in orgasm. Japanese, Indian, French and English all babble about dying ('Some of them,' said Abbé Brantome, 'yell out "I'm dying,"' but I think they enjoy that sort of death'), about Mother (they often call for her at the critical moment) and about religion even if they are atheists. This is natural – orgasm is the most religious moment of our lives, of which all other mystical kicks are a mere translation. Men are apt to growl like bears, or utter aggressive monosyllables like 'In, In, In!' The wife of The Leopard in the novel used to yell out 'Gesumaria!' and there are an infinite variety of sounds short of speech. Why these are so charming in both sexes it's hard to say. The Indians classified them, compared them to bird-cries, and warned how easily parrots and mynahs pick them up, with bad social vibrations when they repeat the lesson – hence no parrots in the love chamber. It is important to learn to read them while enjoying the music, and in particular to know when 'Stop' means stop and when it means 'For God's sake go on.' This is an individual language. You need simply to be a sensitive field observer.

Some of the 'words' are common – a gasp when a touch registers right, a shuddering out-breath when you follow through. Women, and some men, talk continuously in a sort of baby-whisper, or repeat four-letter words of the most unlikely kind – some you can hear several blocks away, while others still are dead silent or laugh or sob disconcertingly. Of the really noisy performers, some like to be allowed to yell, while others like to be gagged, or stuff their hair in their mouths in the style of a Japanese print (Japanese houses have paper partitions). Men can be equally noisy but are not usually so continuously vocal.

BEDS *overleaf*
Still the most important piece of sexual equipment.

The important points are these – in mutual, let-go intercourse, make as much noise as you like. It is curious that we need to write this down, but house and hotel designers haven't yet realized it – they all seem to be married to noiseless, childless partners, or they'd avoid plasterboard. Totally silent intercourse, with each partner's hand firmly over the other's mouth, can be fun if you simply can't risk being overheard. Another variation is to have two kinds of intercourse at once – straight, gentle coitus, while each partner describes some other much wilder proceeding in fantasy, perhaps for next time. The fantasy can be as wild as you like. This is the place to experience things you can't possibly act out, and to learn your partner's fantasy needs. These fantasies can be heterosexual, homosexual, incestuous, tender, wild or bloodthirsty – don't block, and don't be afraid of your partner's fantasy; this is a dream you are in. But be careful about recording such dreams, as they can be disturbing at the daylight level. Let them go with the release of orgasm.

Lovers who really know one another won't be frightened, nor take advantage. If you do find this double nakedness disturbing, set rules – practicable or happy fantasies only; never, never refer to pillow-talk in anger later on ('I always knew you were a lesbian, etc.'). This is contemptible. Fantasy apart, the only really disturbing manifestation of love-music is when the woman laughs uncontrollably – some do. Don't be up-tight about this. She isn't laughing at you.

birth control

This is the discovery which more than any other makes carefree sex possible. Before that one had to be infertile to enjoy the kind of extended sexual play which is now available to everyone who is reasonably housed (and which will eventually be available to everyone, together with control over their fertility). No other method being wholly reliable, women who have once experienced the security of the Pill and discovered the play-function of sex are not going to return to the old insecurity. The Pill is still the safest and best method, and a safer drug than aspirin. The loop, and similar indwelling appliances, which prevent implantation, don't suit everyone but work well for some. If you can't use these, it is back to the cap plus a good chemical spermicide. Some women find capping themselves before sex offputting and complain that half the sensation is lost and they get consumer resistance from their man (though if it is the only method she can use, don't make a song and dance about it; that won't change anything and will make her apprehensive); other women, given privacy and washing facilities, don't mind, though both caps and spermicides can spoil both the feel of the

BIRTH CONTROL *opposite*
The discovery which more than any other makes carefree sex possible.

vagina and the genital odor, but usually not seriously. The man should check with his finger that the cap really is over the cervix as part of loveplay. One point about the Pill is that by turning off the normal acid vaginal secretion, it makes it far easier to catch VD or thrush, even from very slight genital or oral contact.

Condoms still have their uses – for a start the very

manipulation involved in letting the woman put one on her man excites some people: thin or 'gossamer' condoms can slow down some over-quick ejaculators. Uncircumcised men, and men with a pointed rather than round-ended glans, can't usually use the teat-ended kind – in this case ask for the round-ended variety. The various knobbed or otherwise decorated sheaths sold to vary vaginal sensation are not reliable or leakproof as contraceptives (see *Gadgets and Gimmicks*), so don't trust them. See *Rubber*. Many people dislike the feeling of no contact.

Finally, never take a risk. Wanted children can limit the sex play of adults by being around; this is a small price to pay if one does want them, and privacy can usually be arranged. Unwanted children are the one moral and ecological offense which nothing today can excuse. In an emergency douche thoroughly at once with soapy water, put spermicidal foam or jelly well into the vagina, rubbing it over the cervix, and see a sympathetic doctor next day – implantation can usually be prevented. But such emergencies shouldn't arise.

The so-called rhythm method ('Vatican Roulette') doesn't merit serious consideration. Not only is it highly unreliable, but it may well account for the slightly higher incidence of abnormal babies among Catholic users through stale eggs getting fertilized.

clothes

It is part of the recovery from puritanism that most people now make love naked and most lovers sleep naked. Clothes, when they are worn, are there to be taken off – making love can very well start by undressing one another, or by one partner stripping for the other. Womens' magazines and phonograph records now give what amount to courses on burlesk-type stripping as a conventional turn-on for the man, but this use of clothing *is* a conventional routine – for a start, it need not be the woman who strips. Each partner, moreover, should practice removing the clothes of the other sex without clumsiness or hold-ups, and preferably with one hand.

Clothes and their removal as a kick have, if one wants to be serious about it, a whole biology in terms of 'releasers,' a releaser being what turns somebody on. The releasers for the male are garments which emphasize breasts and buttocks or, like tight panties, 'simplify the outline' of the female. Women are not so dependent on this sort of concrete signalling – having the right man is their chief releaser, a social and emotional one – but many of them have preferences. A well-filled jockstrap, or a man naked from the waist down, can act as part of the preliminary scenery, and habitual nudity in bed and about the house doesn't blunt these natural reactions.

Quite apart from this, some people react very strongly to particular clothing-situations on a lock and key basis – usually these are men, occasionally women. This is the

CLOTHES *above*
If your man has a physical turn-on he will love you more the more skillfully you sense and use it.

basis of kinky fashions. Exactly what works on a particular person is highly individual; in this case he often knows and will ask for it. These clothing turn-ons work exactly as a salmon-fly works for the salmon. A bunch of feathers doesn't look like anything the salmon eats (and when one fishes for them at salmon run they aren't feeding in any case) but it combines a whole range of unrelated stimuli which excite curiosity, aggression, and enough other fishy emotions to provoke a strike. Human turn-ons are equally complicated. How they become programmed in a given individual isn't known, but there is an identifiable repertoire of components, like the repertoire of feathers one can use in a lure from which most of these stimuli are made. Super-skin is one – tightness, shininess and texture: super-genitalness – firm pubis, space between the thighs, extra pubic hair; mild threat – blackness, leatheriness, sadistic-looking buckles; submission – tied-upness, slave-bangles; and the suggestion of genitals elsewhere – red lips, emphasis on the feet, which have 'some symmetry with that which thou dost crave;' shininess and tinkling – earrings, chains: woman-ness – tiny waist, big breasts and buttocks, long hair. And so on. Humans love to fool around with the body-image and alter it.

Others are textures – wetness, fur, rubber, plastic, leather. Most males, but fewer females, respond slightly to all of these, and this is another basis of sexual fashion. Some respond so strongly to a few that they don't hit full sexual function without them, but the selection is highly individual, far more so than taste in food, and to tie your fly you have to know your salmon. Every such lure has at least three layers – tight, shiny, black leather is a superskin with a womany smell – it also suggests acceptance of the aggression of sex. Tiny, tight g-strings stress but hide her pussy, hold her perfume so she can be kissed through them, and suggest wicked, sexy girls rather than chaste sister-figures. Corsets make her hourglass-shaped and suggest tightness and helplessness. And so on. A horse, seen from behind, is a male 'releaser'– it has long hair, big buttocks and a teetering walk. A cow isn't.

Prostitutes, who know all this elementary biology, use all these lures, or dress one of them and catch fish who respond to it. Women in love, unless they happen to have similar turn-ons themselves, have long tended to be a bit scared of them as kinky, and, in particular, to feel 'he's in love with gloves or black lingerie, not with me.' This is the wrong approach. If your man has a physical turn-on, it has nothing to do with his valuation of you, and he will love you more the more skillfully you sense and use it. Turn-ons are not choosable – he has them or he hasn't. If he has them, you can catch your favorite fish at every cast. If he likes long hair you'd grow it – you might even

CLOTHES *opposite and overleaf*
If he likes you to look like a cross between a snake and a seal, wear what he gives you. If you like him a particular way, see he knows it.

try to make yourself slim, or blonde, to attract him. You can't make yourself tall, or beautiful, unless you are that way already. But if he has a preference you *can* meet you are unstoppable. The 'you' part is in letting him see you sense it and meet it. If you too have turn-ons, tell him, and use them.

Accordingly, the same tactic applies here as for sexual fantasies generally. Uninhibited partners will tell each other about them (try free-associating just before orgasm if you are shy). Really communicating partners look for them and put them on the menu unannounced – there is no more complete communication. As with other fantasies, if the thing itself doesn't turn you on equally, the response will. Infantile, symbolic, fetishistic and generally wild fantasies are part of love, and only a problem if they take up too much time and start spoiling the full reciprocity of sex (see *Fetishes*). For most people they don't, and a great many people of both sexes have them. No matter how odd, they are usually rewarding – more so than ties or candy as anniversary presents. People are still rightly shy about their innermost mind-life; if your partner seems preoccupied and is blocked over this, ask him or her to give you the thing he or she would most like to see you wearing when you come to lovemaking, and wear it. If you really can't share these essential kids' games or communicate such turn-ons for fear of each other's reactions you shouldn't be in bed together at all. Noncommunication, not normal human fantasy, lands people in the divorce court for incompatibility; a fantasy which really turns you off is subject for discussion and adjustment through make-believe, and just as men tend to be programmed for concrete signals, women are programmed to pick up the kind of signal which turns their partner on – after a few big orgasms together all but the oddest fantasies get to be shared.

So, if he likes you to look like a cross between a snake and a seal, wear what he gives you. If you like him a particular way, see he knows it. Some women are bothered that a man who occasionally likes them to dress him in their clothes is unvirile (it causes less anxiety the other way round). But all of us have a person of the opposite sex inside us – Queen Omphale dressed the hero Hercules in her clothes, and he wasn't exactly unvirile. This is a common game or ceremony in other cultures. We accept sex as pleasure and are starting to accept it as play. Now we need to accept it as ceremony, plus the fact that we are all bisexual and that sex includes fantasy, self-image, psycho-drama, and the other things which our society still finds worrying. Bed is the place to act these things out – that is one of the things human sex is for.

Special preferences apart, it's worth knowing at least

as much as a pro about the common turn-ons, because for most couples they have stunning surprise value as un-scheduled extras on special occasions. If a particular one doesn't work you needn't repeat it, and clothes are easy to take off.

Makers of sexy lingerie cater for honeymoon trous-seaux but don't seem to produce a sexually practicable female g-string. This should tightly cover the whole pussy and pubic hair, nothing else. It should undo from the sides with hooks, or better with ribbons, so that it can be taken off when astride without kicking your man. The traditional 'leaf' worn by Japanese prostitutes is made of silk, not nylon, because it holds your perfume better. See *G-string*. This isn't street wear – you wear it only for sex: the first direct genital kiss is given, or taken, through it. Later you can surprise him by suddenly taking the two ends and putting it hard over his nose and mouth. Men are better catered for, with what are called in Europe 'posing pouches' worn by wouldbe strong-men for near-nude photos. Use these in the same way. Two such minimum g-strings make the ideal nightwear, if you want nightwear.

come again

Not all can, but we are sure that far more could than actually do, men especially.

Multiple orgasm comes easily to many if not all women if they are responsive enough and care to go on, either with intercourse or afterplay, after one orgasm; that is, really responsive women who definitely fall in the once-and-it's-over category like men are fairly rare. Some women get one continuous series of orgasms with no single, big peak. Responsiveness is an unanalyzably subtle mixture of physiology, mood, culture, upbringing and having the man she wants. Therefore, if you can get one really intense climax you could probably get more if you went on. The chief exceptions are those who are fragile and tire easily, or who want to savor the period of intense relaxation after each orgasm rather than switch to a new kind of stimulation.

With men it is more complicated still. Some can get six or more full orgasms in a few hours provided they aren't timestressed and don't attempt it daily. Some can do it daily. Others can't get a second erection for a set time. It pays to establish this time early on – it may be shorter than you think. Whether it is alterable nobody knows – nor yet whether individual differences depend on physical or mental factors, though certainly a great many men have been hocussed by talk about sex being exhausting into a performance below what they could manage.

Since exercise and practice improve almost all per-formances it would be odd if they didn't improve this one.

In any case it's not, for the man, the number of orgasms that matter – most men can get a second by slow hand-work and a third from self-stimulation within an hour of full intercourse – it is rather the ability either to hold off your own orgasm as long as you want, or to go on after, or soon after it, even if you don't come a second time. Failing this one can't take a woman the whole way in unsupplemented intercourse. Many lovers don't try but switch their techniques to economize – yet even so it's not the same unless you manage to finish, if not together, at least fairly close together.

Ability to hold and to repeat is particularly important to the many (usually over-continent) males who have hair-trigger trouble. Don't let it become a self-aggravating worry. It matters not a jot provided you can get another erection inside half an hour – there are plenty of other things to do while you are waiting. Avoid performance anxiety: instead, find out by trial just how soon you can

COME AGAIN *below and opposite* If he can't, doesn't or is worried, it is no use reasoning with him. You, Madam, must take over.

get a serviceable erection again – usually this will be long-lasting and won't end in a full climax, but will enable you to give her ten, twenty or more minutes of full intercourse while you concentrate on her.

If he can't, doesn't, or is worried about it, it is no use reasoning with him. You, Madam, must take over. Full technical details are given under *Hairtrigger trouble*. If you look disappointed you'll have had it for the night and possibly for keeps. Suggest some diversionary entertainment, give him half an hour, then stiffen him yourself by hand and mouth-work. Tell him out of hours what you intend doing; you want to see how soon he can get stiff again (otherwise it looks as though you were unsatisfied and he'll feel guilty and switch himself off). Bring this off neatly and you'll have added a new dimension to both your lives. Two important points – one, *immediately* after a full orgasm some men can't stand any genital stimulation – they feel it as intense pain. If he is like this, give him a half hour or more. Two, if he really is up-tight about it, quite a few women can be perfectly well penetrated with the merest half-erection if taken from behind on their side. Once started like this, full erection usually follows.

Some men when tired can't get an erection but can ejaculate on hand or mouth-work: others get an erection which lasts indefinitely but can't reach orgasm. This last sort, who are actually slow, not fast, responders, make sexual athletes. Whether it can be cultivated as a choice isn't clear, but abundant sex and a certain amount of masturbatory training in holding back a climax will help. Most over-fast responders are having sex far too rarely.

Corpse revivers: the best are skillful manual and oral work and direct suction. A woman can carefully take not only the penis but the whole scrotum as well into her mouth and hold them with her lips, then suck firmly on the penis itself while pressing with a finger at its root behind. Then, when she feels stiffening, she can switch to in and out movements. Vigorous masturbation will always produce a second ejaculation in time, even if it doesn't produce a serviceable erection Some couples, all passion spent, but still wanting one more orgasm before finishing, like to lie facing and watch one another as they bring themselves to climax. This is an added experience, not a confession of defeat, and can be immensely and unexpectedly exciting.

deodorant

Banned absolutely, the only permitted deodorant is soap and water although the unfortunates who sweat profusely may well have problems. A mouthful of aluminium chloride in a girl's armpit is one of the biggest disappointments bed can afford, and a truly deodorized woman would be another – like a deodorized carnation. Cleanliness is another matter. Accordingly, don't give in to sales talk, unless you find that a so-called 'intimate deodorant' enhances a natural note which pleases you. Wash, and leave it at that. She says: 'Some men *should* use deodorants if they can't learn to wash.' See *Cassolette, Mouth music.*

foreskin

Cutting off this structure is possibly the oldest human sexual ritual. It still persists – on the ground, now, either that cancer of the penis and cervix is rarer when it is done (washing probably works as well) or that it slows down orgasm (for which there is no evidence). We're against it, though for some it is already too late. To cut off the uppermost skin of the secret parts,' said Dr. Bulwer, 'is directly against the honesty of nature, and an injurious insufferable trick put upon her.' The point is that if you have a foreskin, you conserve your options. It probably doesn't make very much difference, either to masturbation or to intercourse, but it makes some, and nobody wants to lose a sensitive structure. Normally one retracts it anyway for all these purposes, but if you haven't one there is a whole range of covered-glans nuances you can't recapture. Women who have experienced both are divided – and over which looks sexier. Some find the circumcised glans 'neater' and are even turned off by an unretracted prepuce as looking 'feminine' (this can be an insight into the symbolic wilderness behind the original Stone Age custom), while others love the sense of discovery which goes with retraction. If you are uncircumcised and she prefers the other, retract it – if vice versa, you've had it. In function it's probably a scent-diffusing organ – nothing to do with sensitivity.

Holding the skin back hard with the hand (her hand) during intercourse works for both circumcised and uncircumcised as an accelerator and a sensation of its own (see *Florentine*). Much of the action of various fancy penile rings is in holding back the skin of the shaft and/or the prepuce and giving extra tightness, which is why some men get extra feeling from them. If you think your glans is oversensitive, try keeping it constantly exposed. You can always have the exposure made permanent when you've tried it. In sum, the circumcised man isn't at any important disadvantage (or advantage), but we prefer to be able to choose our egg with or without salt and let our children do likewise.

frequency

The right frequency for sex is as often as you both enjoy it. You can no more 'have too much' sex than you can over-empty a toilet cistern (see *Excesses*) though you can

cut your fertility by having too many ejaculations, and you don't want to make intercourse such an anxious business that you have to stick to a daily schedule. Two or three times a week is a common rate. Many people have it much oftener Some people do stick to a pretty regular schedule – others like intensive weekends at intervals. Much under twice a week suggests you could be getting more out of it, unless you know by experience that the lower frequency is optimal for what you want. People who stick strictly to coital orgasm usually are opting for fewer climaxes than people who mix coitus with oral, manual and other plays, because these increase the number of climaxes most men can get. You should devise your own mix, in the light of your own responses: if one partner needs more, the accessory methods are useful to supply their needs and match them to yours. Frequency falls off normally with age, but there is no age when you won't on some special occasion, surprise yourself. Don't be compulsive about frequency (or worried if your friends say yours is lower than theirs). You aren't being scored. Realize there will be times when one of you just doesn't feel like it – through fatigue, preoccupation, etc.– and don't enforce a timetable on them or yourself.

love

We use the same word for man-woman, mother-child, child-parent, and I-mankind relations – rightly, because they are a continuous spectrum. In talking about sexual relations, it seems right to apply it to any relationship in which there is mutual tenderness, respect and consideration – from a total interdependence where the death of one maims the other for years, to an agreeable night together. The intergrades are all love, all worthy, all part of human experience. Some meet the needs of one person, some of another – or of the same person at different times. That's really the big problem of sexual ethics, and it's basically a problem of self-understanding and of communication. You can't assume that your 'conditions of love' are applicable to, or accepted by, any other party; you can't assume that these won't be changed quite unpredictably in both of you by the experience of loving; you can't necessarily know your own mind. If you are going to love, these are risks you have to take, and don't depend simply on whether or not you have sex together – though that is such a potentially overwhelming experience that tradition is right in pinpointing it. Sometimes two people know each other very well, or think they've worked things out by discussion, and they may be right. But even so if it's dignifiable by the name of love it's potentially an open-ended experience. Tradition has tried to cut the casualties by laying down all kinds of schedules of morality, but these

LOVE *opposite and overleaf*
Sexual love can give us our best and our worst moments.

MEN *opposite*
Male sex response is triggered
easily by things, like putting a
quarter in a vending machine.

never work 100 per cent. Nor are they of much use in classifying the merits of different kinds of relationship. Romantic sentimentalism made a whole generation see 'love' as a kind of take-over bid by one individual for another. Some moderns in revolt from this are, like Casanova, so hung up on no hangups that they won't accept the essential open-endedness of a real relationship between people.

If sexual love can be – and it is – the supreme human experience it must be also a bit hazardous. It can give us our best and our worst moments. In this respect it's like mountain climbing – over-timid people miss the whole experience; reasonably balanced and hardy people accept the risks for the rewards, but realize that there's a difference between this and being foolhardy. Love, moreover, involves someone else's neck beside your own. At least you can make as sure as maybe that you don't exploit or injure someone – you don't take a novice climbing and abandon them halfway up when things get difficult. Getting them to sign a form of consent before they start isn't an answer either. There was a hell of a lot to be said for the English Victorian idea of not being a cad ('person devoid of finer or gentlemanly feelings'). A cad can be of either sex.

Marriage between two rival actor-managers, each trying to produce the other regardless, isn't love. The relationship between a prostitute and a casual client where, for reasons they don't quite get, real tenderness and respect occur, is.

men (by him for her)

Prof. Higgins was right – men wish that women's sexuality was like theirs, which it isn't. Male sexual response is far brisker and more automatic: it is triggered easily by things, like putting a quarter in a vending machine. Consequently, at a certain level and for all men girls, and parts of girls, are at this stimulus level unpeople. That isn't incompatible with their being people too. Your clothes, breasts, odor, etc., aren't what he loves instead of you – simply the things he needs in order to set sex in motion to express love. Women seem to find this hard to understand.

Second, most though not all male feeling is ultimately centered in the last inch of the penis (though you can, if you start intelligently, teach him female-type sensitivity all over his skin surface). And unlike yours his sexuality depends on a positive performance – he has to be turned on to erection, and not turned off, in order to function; he can't be passively 'taken' in a neutral way. This matters intensely to men at a biological and personal level. It explains why men are emphatically penis centered and tend to start with genital play, probably before you are ready, and when you would rather wait to get in the mood.

Genital approach is how men get into the mood.

You need to understand these reactions, as he needs to understand yours. The Women's Lib bit about sex objects misses the point – sure the woman and the various parts of her are sex objects, but most men ideally would wish to be treated piecemeal in the same way. Accordingly, the most valued thing, from you, in actual love-making is intuition of these object reactions and direct initiative – *starting* the plays, taking hold of the penis, giving genital kisses ahead of being asked – being an initiator, a user of your stimulatory equipment. This is hard to put into simple terms; it is what John Wilkes meant by the divine gift of lechery – the art of sensing turn-ons and going along with them for the partner's response. It isn't the same for the two sexes because male turn-ons are concrete, while many female turn-ons are situational and atmospheric. Personal folklore apart, what the male turn-on equipment requires is the exact reverse of a virgin or a passively recipient instrument – not a demand situation, because that in itself can threaten a turn-off from inadequacy-feelings, but a skill situation; I can turn you on and turn myself on in doing so, and from that point we play it both ways and together. You can't of course control your turn-ons any more than he can, but it helps if a woman has some male-type object reactions, like being excited by the sight of a penis, or hairy skin, or by the man stripping, or by physical kinds of play (just as it helps if the man has some sense of atmosphere). It's the active woman who understands his reactions while keeping her own who is the ideal lover.

naked apes

We put a lot of biology into this book; too much exposition has been devoted to symbolisms in human sex behavior, highly important as these are, from a psychoanalytic standpoint which assumes, like old-style morality, that there is only one way of making love and only one thing it ought to express. Work on monkeys suggests that for man the possibility of prolonged and sensuous sex is something special, i.e. a 'displacement activity,' which enables all kinds of aggressions and anxieties as well as infant deprivation of skin sensation, to be worked out play-fashion in the context of mutual affection. Most people have at least one preferred sex behavior which a judge would find odd. If we saw these behaviors in fish or birds we wouldn't ask whether they were normal, but what they were for. No writer who has watched apes should say, as one did recently, that any voluntary movement in sexual intercourse is evidence of latent sadism – if it is, then 'latent sadism' means using sex to dissipate natural aggression in play. Problems only arise when the natural play-function isn't able to dissipate deeper anxieties.

Man's chief differences from most apes are pair-formation, the extensive use of sex as social bonding and play, shift of interest from brightly-colored buttocks to breasts (one baboon has this too) and imagination. Well-known ape residues are blushing – all that is left of the mandril's red facial sex-skin (it happens all over to many women in orgasm, as a spotty-looking rash), and persisting buttock interest, which may include reddening them by smacking. Worth knowing only because sex is more fun, and preferences less alarming, if they make sense as natural history. Apes, like men, masturbate and play bi-sexual games.

nakedness

The normal state for lovers who take their work at all seriously, at least as a basic requisite – subject to the reservations under *Clothes*. They don't so much start clothed and shed what they must, as start naked and add any extras they need.

Nakedness doesn't mean lack of ornament. The oriental lady takes off all her clothes but puts on all her jewels – the only practical need, as with wrist watches, is to see they don't catch or scratch. This is for daylight; it is difficult to sleep in them. For night, probably increase in the value of lovemaking is the main reason that most people now sleep naked. The only exception may be after; warm bodies tend to stick, and a blotter worn by one or other can add to comfort. We find we spend more and more of our time together naked or wearing the en-hancing minimum. It affects our choice of clothes and of, for example, nonclammy chairs.

Nudists, incidentally, used to be a dead loss – there are no pants like invisible pants. Now, thank goodness, the swingers and, better, the uninhibited young are moving in, for whom nudity is natural not a ritual and lovemaking is included, instead of eurhythmics or basketball – or as well.

Organized 'nudism' in most countries is a family affair. This is probably a good idea. For biological reasons which we've hinted at elsewhere (see *Penis, Vulva, Children*) the nudity of one's own parents can be worrying to children, and shouldn't be overdone. Children of militant pro-gressives often develop disconcerting modesty, which should be respected even if nakedness at home comes naturally. There is accordingly a lot to be said for the op-portunity to look at men and women in general under un-forced conditions and without programmed incest and dominance anxieties: not 'father is bigger than I am' but 'all men are bigger than I am, and one day I shall be a man.' It is the discharge of residual adult anxiety of this sort about our acceptability and competitive status which

NAKEDNESS   *overleaf*
The normal state for lovers who take their work at all seriously.

probably makes group nudity so relaxing, rather than the opportunity of getting sunburned, and explains why it acts as a lay sacrament. Career nudists at a first meeting do have the openness of hippies or Quakers, though they quarrel a fair amount over dogma. You can pick a square or a swinging club to taste – they at least give facilities for prolonged open-air nakedness which are hard to organize at home.

normal

A nineteenth-century book about sex, unless it was meant for the (then rich) underground would have started with at least a genuflection to what was and wasn't sinful. The next generation of medical books, and much counseling literature, switched to laying down rules about what is and isn't normal.

Tack 'abnormal' onto a sexual taste and it becomes worrying. 'Normal' implies that there is something which sex ought to be. There is. It ought to be a wholly satisfying link between two affectionate people, from which both emerge unanxious, rewarded and ready for more. That definition includes the awareness that people differ wildly in what they need and in their capacity to be satisfied; more, statistically, than in almost any other measurable. Since sex is cooperative you can cater to one another alternately to bridge gaps. Add to this that sex, for reasons built into the species, makes us uniquely anxious compared with other divergences of need or taste and our culture is coming out of a period of moral panic into a re-awareness that there is nothing to fear. Accordingly, a lot of people are, in their sexual assumptions, like the generation of Victorian children brought up to believe that green sweets were poisonous and rice pudding was good for you because it was unpalatable: they need reassuring.

One trouble with the last generation was that because of censorship by Auntie, many good sex techniques were simply unfamiliar, and worrying or disgusting for that reason. It is not much over a lifetime ago that Krafft-Ebing wrote a textbook in which he described every sexual routine he didn't himself enjoy as a named 'disease,' salting the narrative with examples drawn from very disturbed people. Even Freud, who recognized that all of us have not one but a whole sheaf of sexually important drives – so much so that nearly all our interests have *some* sexual overtone – regarded maturity in terms of a pretty rigid highway code. There was practically an examination in 'maturity' to take at the end.

'Abnormal' accordingly means (1) unusual for the time and place – having intercourse ten times a day on a regular basis is unusual but it happens. If you can, fine. Leonardo and Newton were statistically unusual. (2) Un-

PENIS *opposite*
Lovers treat the penis as **something very like a third party.**

usual and disapproved. It's abnormal in Papua to bury dead relatives, and abnormal in California to eat them. Yet lovers all over the world would like 'to eat' one another, and the same idea underlies our most beautiful and moving religious rite. At the same time an Englishman or an American who actually ate a dead relative would have to be pretty sick. On a less extreme level, our society is scared of same-sex affection. In classical Greece it was a fashionable pose – everyone did it who could. In our culture the people who show exclusively this sort of response are those who must. (3) Unusual and handicapping. A slipped disk or a really worrying sexual obsession are abnormalities because they spoil life, for the owner and his or her associates.

Some sex behaviors are obviously odd, and restrict the range of enjoyment – like the man who could only get orgasm by getting into a bath of cooked spaghetti. He, however, liked it that way. Psychologists now do not usually ask 'Is this normal?' but 'Why does this particular person need this particular emphasis?' and 'Is this behavior, (a) spoiling his chances of being a full person, (b) tolerable for society?' Some, like rape or seducing children, obviously aren't tolerable.

In sum, we don't have a single 'normal' pattern of sex behavior, but a bunch of responses, like the fingers of a hand. In most people in a given culture fingers are of roughly the same lengths. Some people have one finger longer than usual – a few are unlucky enough to have one long finger and the others stunted. The difference here is that finger lengths are much more tightly programmed and vary much less than sex behaviors. Accordingly, if you must talk about 'normality,' any sex behavior is normal which (1) you both enjoy, (2) hurts nobody, (3) isn't associated with anxiety, (4) doesn't cut down your scope. Insisting on having intercourse only in the dark, in one position, and with as little pleasure as possible, which used to be the moralists' stereotype of normality, is a very anxious and limiting routine. Good, unworried lovers use all five fingers of all four hands.

penis

More than the essential piece of male equipment, even if it is often and expressively described as a 'tool,' the penis has more symbolic importance than any other human organ, as a dominance signal and, by reason of having a will of its own, generally a 'personality.' No point in reading all this symbolism back here, except to say that lovers will experience it, and find themselves treating the penis as something very like a third party. At one moment it is a weapon or a threat, at another something they share, like a child. Without going into psychoanalysis or biology it's not a bad test of a love-relationship that while the penis is emphatically his, it also belongs to both of them. This particular set of programmed feelings in man is in fact the fine adjustment for all manner of experiences and feelings connected with sex-roles, identity and development. Freud's formulation, that the man is programmed to fear that the woman, or a jealous parent, will confiscate his penis, while the woman feels it is something she has lost, is biologically true but over-simple. What is true is that in a good sex scene it becomes their' penis. In any case its texture, erectility and so on are fascinating to both sexes, and its apparent autonomy a little alarming. This is programmed, and the fact that the human penis is much bigger relatively than in other primates is probably due to these complex psychological functions: it's an aesthetic as well as a functional object.

For precisely the same reasons it collects anxieties and folklore, and is a focus for all sorts of magical manipulations. Male self-esteem and sense of identity tend to be located in it, as Samson's energy was in his hair. If it won't work, or worse, if you as a woman send it up, or down, the results will be disastrous. This explains the irrational male preoccupation with penile size. Size has absolutely nothing to do with their physical serviceability in inter-

PLAYTIME *above*
The rules are only those of childplay—if it gets nasty or spiteful, stop the game.

course, or – since female orgasm doesn't depend on getting deeply into the pelvis – with capacity to satisfy a partner, though many women are turned on by the idea of a large one, and a few say that they feel more. The un-stretched vagina is only 4 inches long anyway. If anything, thickness matters more. Nor has flaccid size anything to do with erect size – a penis which is large when at rest simply enlarges less with erection. There is no way of 'en-larging' a penis. Size doesn't differ appreciably between 'races,' nor correlate with big muscles elsewhere. Nor, ex-cept in very rare cases, is a penis too big for a woman – the vagina will take a full-term baby. If your penis, whatever its length, hits an ovary and hurts her, don't go in so far. A woman who says she is 'too small' or 'too tight' is making a statement about her worries, exactly as the man who is obsessed with being too small. They need reassurance and a different attitude to sex, not gadgets or exercises. Shape also varies – the glans can be blunt or conical. This matters only in that the conical shape can make teat-ended con-doms uncomfortable through getting jammed in the teat. As to circumcision and uncircumcision, its effects are religious rather than sexual, see *Foreskin*. If you have anxious preconceptions, get rid of them. All the preceding statements are true.

Women who have really learned to enjoy sex are usually as fascinated by their lover's penis, size included, as men are by women's breasts, shape, odor and feel, and learn to play with it fully and skillfully. Circumcised or not, it's a fascinating toy quite apart from experiencing its main use. There is a whole play scene connected with uncap-ping, stiffening, and handling it, making it pulsate or ejacu-late, which is a major part of togetherness. This is equally important for the man – not only is it ego-boosting, but good hand and mouth work practically guarantee a good partner.

Care and maintenance: if you aren't circumcised, you need to retract the foreskin fully for cleaning purposes, and if it won't retract beyond the corona all round the glans except at the front, get it seen to (this is a trifling operation with a blunt probe and doesn't necessarily mean you need circumcising). If it won't retract properly or is over-tight and gets stuck, get that seen to also. These are about the only things that are commonly wrong with a penis. Slight asymmetry often develops with time – this does no harm. On the other hand don't bend an erect penis, or use a position in which it could get violently bent by accident. (This usually happens with the woman on top if she is care-less near orgasm, or in putting him in, and he is just short of fully stiff – keep a little control here.) It is possible, though difficult, to fracture one of the two hydraulics con-

PLAYTIME *overleaf*
sex is the most important sort of
adult play. If you can't relax here
you never will.

tained in the shaft. This is very painful and can lead to pain or kinking on subsequent erection. For the same reason avoid silly tricks with tubes, suction or 'enlarging' devices. The normal organ will stand up to extremely hard use, but not to these. Sores, discharge, etc., are illnesses and need treatment. Venereal disease apart, don't have oral intercourse with someone who has a herpes on the mouth – you can get recurrent herpes of the penis or the vulva which is a nuisance. If the foreskin is dry from masturbation or long retraction, saliva is the best lubricant unless you have a herpes yourself. Penile cosmetics are now sold – some are deodorants, others local anaesthetics to slow down response, and yet others ticklers. We don't recommend them.

playtime

We have said this before, but we repeat : sex is the most important sort of adult play. If you can't relax here you never will. Don't be scared of psychodrama. It works far better in bed than in an encounter group – be the Sultan and his favorite concubine, the burglar and the maiden, even a dog and a currant bun, anything you fancy for the hell of it. Take off your shell along with your clothes.

A few people are immensely excited by having sex with the assistance of the oldest human dramatic expedient, a mask – which suppresses you and makes you someone else (see *Masks*). Most of us can learn to do the same change without it, and when this comes the complete mental nakedness between you is the most exhilarating sort of nudism – so complete that one is healthily scared of it at first. Getting unscared is probably the most important lesson of sex. One Martini helps – more can spoil it. Real sex release when one achieves it is what alcohol, pot, etc., are substitutes *for*, however.

So let him be a Roman or a dog or a woman or a gangster, and let her be a virgin, or a slave, or a Sultana, or Lolita, or someone you're trying to rape, or indeed anything which turns either of you on. You weren't self-conscious about this when you were three – grow backwards again in an adult context. The rules are only those of childplay – if it gets nasty or spiteful or unhappy, stop the game : while it stays wild and exciting, it has a climax childrens' games lack; that is the privilege of adult play.

pubic hair

Shave it off if you prefer : we don't, but some people do. If you do once shave it, you're committed to a prickly interregnum while it regrows. Some prefer it off in the interest of total nudity or prefer the hardness of the bare pubis – most find it decorative. Most lovers regard pubic hair as a resource. Try brushing it lightly and learn to caress with it.

It can be combed, twirled, kissed, held, even pulled. In the woman it can move the whole pubis, skillfully handled, to the point of orgasm. For the woman, it's often best not to shave but to trim, confining the triangle to the middle of the pubis with a bare strip each side – the pattern of youth – removing hair which comes outside a g-string or bathing slip, and trimming enough to make the vulva fully visible. Better not try to dye it to match head hair – it never looks right – still less to bleach it. *M.A.S.H.* is quite wrong – you can't tell whether a blonde is natural by her pubic hair color. It is often shades darker than head hair – in black-haired women it can be nearly blue. Men can shave if they like, or their partners like, but it's difficult to shave the scrotum. Don't use depilatories around the genitals – they can burn. You may need to shave the penile shaft and root if you use a condom – otherwise the hairs can get rolled into it.

real sex

The sort our culture and most admass propaganda don't recognize: not that intercourse or masturbation or genital kisses aren't real sex, but some other things are real sex too, which people need, but which don't excite our time and age. We can list some: being together in a situation of pleasure, or of danger, or just of rest (if we admitted these as sexual we'd run the risk of having to love other people as people, and that would be worrying or inconvenient, to us or society): touching: oldfashioned expedients like holding hands (permissiveness makes more orgasms, but we miss out on old-style restricted courtship, kisses and looks that vagina-bent, with-it males now think of as schmalz): sleeping together even without, or especially after, intercourse.

Most women don't need telling this, but are as shy about telling it to males, for fear of seeming square, as males are about object-preferences or aggressive needs. Don't get stuck with the view that only those things which Auntie calls sexual are sexual. In a book on sexual elaboration, this needs saying, if you are concerned with love rather than an Olympic pentathlon. People in our culture who are hung up on the Olympic bit don't get much from it unless it helps them to learn this.

relaxation

It is probably the general experience, and we have been assuming here, that maximum feeling in orgasm goes with maximum muscular tension. A great many techniques (postures, bondage and so on) are designed to boost this tension. On the other hand, it is by no means universally true. The orgasm of total relaxation is rather harder to manage, largely because it cannot be boosted artificially, but is both different and, when it works, overwhelming. There are also some people, chiefly women, for whom tension seems actively to interfere with full response.

We've seen ideological writings about this which infer, for example, that tension-orgasms represent fear of full release, latent sadism and so on. One writer opined that yells, grimaces and convulsions indicate fear and pain rather than love and pleasure – presumably he had never seen himself making love, or had never had a wild orgasm. In fact, the only universal generalization about sex seems to be that no one pattern fits everyone. How far these differences between people depend on physiology and how far on latent aggression and the like is probably not a practically important question – some need one and some the other. Our point is that with practice most people can widen their repertoire by learning to use both, and sense the needs of the moment so as to alternate them, thereby doubling their range of physical sensation and making sex still more communicative. Certainly some tension represents fear of letting-go, and some people prefer to be 'forced,' voluntarily, to accept orgasms – in this case,

PUBIC HAIR   *opposite*
Better not try to dye it to match head hair – it never looks right.

initially at least, it's probably sensible to make use of the responses you have. If you recognize this kind of reaction, however, don't omit to try the other mode. Mammals seem to vary, according to species, between fight-and-rape-type mating and a version in which the female appears near-indifferent, so there isn't much to be learned from zoology.

The straight, sleepy, non-special intercourse, on your side or in the matrimonial position, is relaxed, but this isn't what we mean. In going for a fully relaxed orgasm, either one partner is totally passive and the other a soloist, or both achieve a state of non-effort in which wholly automatic movements – internal, for the woman – take over. Try both kinds – it is easier initially to work up both modes together.

Probably the easiest initial method is for the less-active partner in ordinary intercourse (this usually but not always means the one underneath) to try stopping all movement just as the orgasmic buildup begins and go completely limp (warn your partner first). Some people do this naturally: if you have had any of the fashionable relaxation training, starting by letting one finger get heavy and so on, use the same technique here. You may find that on the first few occasions the fact of trying produces a different sort of tension, but after a few attempts most easily-stimulated people can learn to let their orgasm happen, and will find that this feels different from the equally pleasant orgasm one produces, either by trying or by struggling and postponing. Don't postpone – don't, in fact, be active at all. Then practice the same kind of relaxation while your partner masturbates or sucks you. The movements he or she makes will be physically the same as for 'slow masturbation' as we've described it, but the operator is looking for quite different feedback – in the 'hard' version, whether the partner is tied or free, you are deliberately holding back or forcing them on, keeping just that much out of step with their reactions. In the 'soft' version you need to be a fraction ahead of those reactions so that they don't need to move or struggle. The difference can't be described, only felt. Practically, it means a quicker, steadier rhythm of stimulation – no slow teasing and no sudden bursts – you are making it and they are letting it happen.

Once you have got this right in intercourse and in other kinds of stimulation, including all the extras we've mentioned, you can go on to complete 'motionless' coitus. It won't of course initially be entirely motionless, but try, after the first round of gentle movement, what happens if you stop thinking. Movements of a sort will continue, but in time and with practice get less and less voluntary, especially if the woman has good vaginal

REAL SEX *opposite*
Permissiveness makes more orgasms, but we miss out on old-style courtship.

muscle control. Ultimately, some people learn to insert and do nothing, but still reach an orgasm in which they totally fuse, giving a sensation of being a single person – not describable, again, and probably not always realizable, but fantastic when it happens. We should stress that this doesn't involve going slow, holding back, or any other voluntary intervention. If you find it not working, switch back to ordinary movements, but without taking too much thought – sometimes you will both sense that the moment has come to shift position and go all out for a big one; complete fusion isn't biddable, and ordinary, athletic sex is fine. If, on the other hand, it does happen you will want to repeat it.

Reliable relaxation, and the almost frightening self-loss that goes with it, are what most sexual yogis have aimed at, except that they usually tried not to ejaculate. Some of these sexual mystics recommend a special relaxed posture (man on his left side, girl on her back at right-angles, knees drawn up, legs bridging his hips, feet flat on the bed). Whether this helps may well depend on your build. What is worth suggesting, even for people who can't totally relax, is that they play through all the techniques we have described, aiming at relaxation instead of maximum tension, and adjusting their feedback accord-

RELAXATION *above*
Essential if you hope to go as far in making love communicate as you are physically and mentally able.

ingly. Similarly people who naturally relax in intercourse should try occasionally to play it for full tension – just as women who like to thrash around should sometimes try being forcibly held still, and vice versa. This sort of experimentation against one's built-in response is better value in widening one's range of lovemaking than mechanical variations of posture or trying out gadgets and stunts. It is one part of lovemaking which requires effort beyond mere curiosity, but it's essential if you hope to go as far in making sex communicate as you are physically and mentally able.

semen

There is no lovemaking without spilling this, on occasions at least. You can get it out of clothing or furnishings either with a stiff brush, when the stain has dried, or with a diluted solution of sodium bicarbonate. If you spill it over each other, massage it gently in – the pollen-odor of fresh semen is itself an aphrodisiac, which is why the smell of fresh grass or thalictrum flowers turns most people on. If you want a very copious ejaculate, he can masturbate nearly, but not quite, to orgasm about an hour beforehand to increase prostate secretion.

size

Preoccupation with the size of their genitals is as built-in biologically to men (it is a 'dominance signal,' like a deer's antlers) as sensitivity about their breasts and figure is to women. That, however, is its only importance. The 'average' penis is about 6 inches overall when erect and about $3\frac{1}{2}$ inches round, but penises come in all sizes – larger ones are spectacular but no more effective except as visual stimuli. Smaller ones work equally well in most positions. Accordingly, excessive preoccupation with size is an irrational anxiety, on which quacks batten – one can't increase it, any more than one can increase stature. Girls should learn not to comment on it except favorably, for fear of creating a lasting hang-up – men should learn not to give it a second thought. The few cases where male genitalia are really infantile go with major gland disturbances and are treatable but rare.

The same applies to vaginal size. No woman is too small – if she is, it is due to inability to relax, or a tough hymen. The normal vagina stretches to accommodate a full-term baby – and a tight woman gives the man extra intense feelings. Nor is any vagina too large – if it seems a loose fit, switch to a posture in which her thighs are pressed together. Genital anatomy probably fixes which postures work best for a given couple, but not more than that. With rare exceptions, men and women are universally adapted.

Non-erect size in the male is equally unimportant – some men before erection show no penile shaft at all, but

extend to full size easily. The same applies to testicle weight – it varies, as does nose or mouth size, but has little to do with function. Small genitals are usually due to active muscles in the under-skin layer – a cold bath will shrink the best-endowed male down to Greek statue proportions. The only practical exception is that with a very big penis and a very small woman she should be careful on top, or she will knock an ovary (which feels as a man feels if you knock a testicle) and he shouldn't thrust too hard until he knows he won't hurt her. As to the size of other structures, such as breasts, these may be individual turn-ons, but every build has its sexual opportunities built-in: use them.

tenderness

This, in fact, is what the whole book is about. It doesn't exclude extremely violent games (though many people neither need nor want these), but it does exclude clumsiness, heavyhandedness, lack of feedback, spitefulness and non-rapport generally. Shown fully in the way you touch each other. What it implies at root is a constant awareness of what your partner is feeling, plus the knowledge of how to heighten that feeling, gently, toughly, slowly or fast, and this only comes from an inner state of mind between you. No really tender person can just turn over and go to sleep. Many if not most inexperienced men, and some women, are just naturally clumsy – either through haste, through anxiety, or through lack of sensing how the other sex feels. Men in general are harder-skinned than women – don't grab breasts, stick fingers into the vagina, handle female skin as if it was your own, or (and this goes for both sexes) misplace bony parts of your anatomy. More girls respond to very light than to very heavy stimulation – just brushing pubic or skin hairs will usually do far more than a whole-hand grab. At the same time don't be frightened – neither of you is made of glass. Women by contrast often fail to use enough pressure, especially in handwork, though the light, light variety is a sensation on its own. Start very gently, making full use of the skin surface, and work up. Stimulus toleration in any case increases with sexual excitement until even hard blows can become excitants (though not for everyone). This loss of pain sense disappears almost instantly with orgasm, so don't go on too long, and be extra gentle as soon as he or she has come.

If we could *teach* tenderness most of this book would be superseded by intuition. If you are really heavy-handed, we agree with a recent book which suggests a little practice with inanimate surfaces, dress fastenings and so on. Male strength is a turn-on in sex, but it isn't expressed in clumsy handwork, bear-hugs and brute force – at least not as starters. If there is a problem here, remember you

TENDERNESS *opposite*
Shown fully in the way you touch each other.

both can talk. Few people want to be in bed on any terms with a person who isn't basically tender, and most people are delighted to be in bed with the right person who is.

The ultimate test is whether you can bear to find the person there when you wake up. If you are actually pleased, then you're onto the right thing.

variety

Plan your menus. Nobody wants a seven-course meal every time. At least seventy-five percent of really rewarding sex will be your absolutely straight, bedtime or morning, pattern. For longer sessions you need to be rested – weekends, holidays and special occasions on impulse. If you make up your mind that over the course of time you'll try everything and have sex everywhere, the occasions will arise: when you feel one coming on, or know you will have the opportunity, plan together with the book if you like, but don't expect necessarily to keep to what you outlined. Stick to it sometimes, however, so you don't miss things. Most couples will strike out perhaps a third of our suggestions as not turning them on, and pick up three or four headed 'We must try that,' if they haven't already.

Usually start with vaginal sex, move on to handwork, use mouth-work to get a further erection – maybe have a final orgasm by masturbating together. Prolonged spin-outs involving makebelieve, experiments and so on often go best on waking fresh – so do positions needing a very hard erection. Unlike a man, an untired and responsive woman can afford to take orgasms from any source in any order, unless her pattern is one overwhelming orgasm only – if so, keep it for last. See *Come again*. Varying times of day is well worthwhile but depends on your commitments and how far you can get privacy or clear your mind of other things, but try never to put it off if you both want it, except to 'save up' for something. Planning and thinking about sex to come is part of love. So is lying together in complete luxury afterwards.

virginity

Have a bit of respect for this. The first time doesn't so much 'matter more' to a woman than to a man, but it matters differently. If you find yourself getting into bed with a girl who is a virgin on only a few hours or minutes acquaintance, you're going too fast for both of you. For a start, she's unlikely to be baby-proof: stay with the non-coital extras until you're both quite sure you know what you are doing. Cutting notches is irresponsible. Whatever you do be gentle and slow, as she's bound to be tense and nervous – even if she doesn't look it.

Girls who are virgins will usually say (you can't tell reliably by inspection) and a loving man will ask – men don't

VULVA *opposite*
Lovers should learn early on to watch each other masturbate.

usually advertise the fact. However experienced he seems, the idea should be in the back of the woman's mind that this could be the first time and he may need help: if you're critical or disappointed you could do real mischief. If you're both virgins, you are starting from scratch – don't hurry it.

There's usually no physical problem over first intercourse if you're careful (see *Defloration*) – the commonest is simply male over-eagerness or nervousness (see *Impotence*). If there are problems, get them dealt with at once.

vulva

'The part of you,' as the advertisement says, 'that is most girl,' but also as magic as the penis, and to children, primi-

WOMEN *opposite*
It matters to them who is doing what, far more than it does to most men.

VULVA *below*
As magic as the penis, and to children, primitives and males generally, slightly scarey.

tives and males generally, slightly scarey: it looks like a castrating wound and bleeds regularly, it swallows the penis and regurgitates it limp, it can probably bite and so on. Luckily, few of these biologically programmed anxieties survive closer acquaintance, but they are the origins of most male hangups including homosexuality. Primitives and prudes treat it as if it was radioactive –'all magic,' said a Papuan wizard, 'radiates from it as fingers do from a hand,' and a lot of female put-downs throughout history grew from this kind of Freudian undergrowth.

Sensitive in all its parts – the phallic-minded male is inclined to make a reassuring rush for the clitoris. Lovers should learn early on to watch one another masturbate – few women enjoy excessive clitorial emphasis at the start. Length of labia, size and tightness of the opening make little difference to performance – position relative to the male pubic bone makes more: some lovers only get really good apposition in one or two postures, though usually the tension produced by movement and pulling on the labia in intercourse more than makes up for this. Normally slightly moist, or women would squeak when they walk, and, of course, wets more or less copiously with sexual excitement. Any staining or offensive discharge indicates infection (usually with trichomonads or yeasts) in the vagina, and needs treating. The normal vulval odor varies greatly between women and between times, but should always be pleasant and sexually exciting.

Whether or not your lover has ever explored a woman's pussy in detail, with fingers, eyes and tongue, make sure he explores yours. Learn to kiss it – you have two mouths to his one.

For care and maintenance see *Bidet, Cassolette, Menstruation*. Don't as a rule douche – wash.

Hide-and-seek with the woman's pubic triangle is one of the oldest human games. See *Clothing, Chastity belt*. Cultivate the cunning use of a really practical g-string.

waking

She says: 'Sleep patterns matter, and it's the man who wakes with an erection. While it's great to be woken with intercourse, this doesn't apply when one has had a ghastly day and has an interview coming up next morning; use some sense. It also doesn't apply in the middle of a dream one has to finish.' Some women take minutes or hours to wake up, and though they enjoy gentle intercourse waking – and it works far better than an alarm clock – don't expect athletics. The trouble is that this is the time when many males are ready for them and expect to be ridden, masturbated, sucked and what have you. Keep these early waking workouts for Sundays and holidays and preferably make coffee first, erection or no erection. Some people are lucky in having roughly the same sleeping hours, but if one were early and the other a night person that too could well give rise to real problems. If you have these, talk about them; some people do use sleep as an excuse for avoiding intercourse, but between lovers who are on different clocks it can be real and doesn't imply rejection.

If you have children, you have to be ready to be woken by them, and restrict yourselves accordingly. Don't lock them out. Rearrange your sex life to get the necessary privacy at other times – if all else fails get a baby-sitter and stay at a motel once a month. The sound and fury of really ongoing sex would give primal scene problems to any small child, so don't take risks; the sort of sex we have, and are talking about here, almost excludes fertility – it's a choice one may have to make, while houses and family-structure are as they are.

women (by her for him)

Women, like men, have direct physical responses, sure, but these *are* different (breasts and skin first, please, not a direct grab at the clitoris) and can't be short-circuited. It matters to them who is doing what, far more than it does to most men. The fact that, unlike you, we can't be visibly turned off and lose erection often confuses men into hurrying things or missing major resources. It isn't true that nudity, erotica, etc., don't excite women – probably the difference is that they aren't overriding things. Is it fair, I wonder, to give a simple instance? You can make orgiastically satisfactory love with a near stranger in half an hour flat. But please don't think for that reason that you can do the same for a woman who loves you personally if at the end of the half-hour you put her into a taxi with a bunch of roses and go off to a wife. Granted this, however, there are common reactions.

We seem to be less heavily programmed than you for specific turn-ons, but once we see one of these working on a man we care about, we soon program it into our own response, and can be less rigid and more experimental *because* of this ability. Often if women seem underactive it's because they're scared of doing the wrong thing with that particular man, like touching up his penis when in fact he's trying not to ejaculate – *tell* us if you see us at a loss. The penis isn't a 'weapon' for us so much as a shared possession, rather like a child – it's less the size than its personality, unpredictable movements, and moods which make up the turn-on (which is why rubber dummies are so sickening). Another important thing is the tough-tender mixture: obviously strength is a turn-on, but clumsiness (elbows in eyes, twisted fingers, etc.) is the dead opposite. You never get anywhere by clumsy brutality; however brutal good lovemaking sometimes *looks*, the turn-on is strength-skill-control, not large bruises: and the ability to be tender with it. Some people ask 'Tough or tender?' but the mood shifts so fast you've got to be able to sense it. Surely it's possible – because some lovers do it – to read this balance from the feel of the woman. No obsessive views about reciprocity – who comes on top, etc., does in fact even out during the passing of time: there can be long spells when one enjoys and is happy to let him do the work, and others when you need to control everything yourself and take an extra kick from seeing how you make him respond.

Women aren't 'masochistic' any more than men – if they've knuckled under in the past it's only through social pressures. If they're sadistic, they unfortunately don't reify it like a man and act it out in bed by wearing spurs and cracking a whip (any girl who does this is doing it as a male turn-on): they're more likely to express it as no-saying or nagging, which contributes to nobody's orgasm. Men have a real advantage here in the constructive use of play (and can help women to reify). Since we all have some aggressions, good sex can be wildly violent but still never cruel. A little frightening helps some people sometimes. Anyhow the old idea of man as raper and woman as rapee being built-in is contrary to all experience in a world where role-swapping is general.

As to the Women's Lib bit, nobody can possibly be a good lover – or a whole man – if he doesn't regard women as (a) people and (b) equals. That is really all there is to be said.

Our sense of smell is the keener – don't oversaturate early on with masculine odors; just before orgasm is probably the time for full odor contact. Our own smell excites us as well as yours.

The sort of hand and mouth-work which men like varies enormously. Some like it very rough, some hate it anything but extremely gentle, others in between. There is no way for a woman to tell except by asking and being told – so it's up to the man to say what he likes or he may get the opposite.

Some men are extraordinarily passive, or unimaginative, or inhibited, and – oddly – when they are any of these things, we do not become correspondingly aggressive. We may long to do things and feel thoroughly frustrated, but we won't dare show it in most case . So a woman's love-making will only be good with a good lover and, more important, she will resent any man who is unexciting, not only because it is unexciting but also because she will know she has been unexciting too.

Finally, just as all women are more alike to a man than all men are to a woman, women probably really do differ sexually rather more than men, because of the greater complexity of their sexual apparatus (breasts, skin and so on as well as pussy). Never assume you don't need to relearn for each person. This is true for women with a new man, but perhaps a little less so.

Main
Courses
which everyone needs

bidet

This article of European bathroom furniture is beginning to be trendy in America. It used to be necessary when post-coital douching was the rule, but the Pill has altered that. For washing it can be useful, for example after anal intercourse or cleaning your feet, and less trouble than a shower, though a woman showering looks better than sitting on a bidet like a battery hen. Indiscriminate douching is medically a bad idea in any case – the vagina is self-cleansing and water merely upsets its natural hygiene. Keep the douche, and the bidet, for cleaning-up after menstrual periods.

breasts

'In our maturer years,' wrote Darwin, 'when an object of vision is presented to us which bears any similitude to the form of the female bosom . . . we feel a general glow of delight which seems to influence all our senses, and if the object be not too large we experience an attraction to embrace it with our lips as we did in early infancy the bosom of our mothers.' Alfred Perlès greeted a socialite who was seated next him at dinner with the words 'Those aren't bad – fish them out and let's have a look at them!' Breasts are the natural second target, but often the first one we reach. Just how sensitive they are, in men as well as in women, varies enormously – size is unimportant, as with other sexual organs. Some don't answer at all, even in the emphatically non-frigid; some answer to extremely gentle touches, some to very rough handling (but they are sensitive structures – don't let your residual anger at having been weaned get the better of your commonsense).

Round and round the nipple with the tongue tip or the glans, soft kneading with both hands, gentle biting and sucking gently like a baby are the best gambits. She can use these on the man, plus very gentle fingertip friction – men's nipples easily get sore, however. If her breasts are big enough to meet, one can get a surprising degree of mutuality from intermammary intercourse. This is a good expedient on occasions when she is closed to the public. Lay her half flat on pillows, kneel astride (big toe to her clitoris if she needs helping) and your foreskin fully retracted. Either you or she can hold the breasts together – wrap them around the shaft rather than rub the glans with them. It should protrude clear, just below her chin. An orgasm from this position, if she gets one, is 'round' like a full coital orgasm, and she feels it inside. Breast orgasms from licking and handling are 'in between' in feel. Rub the semen well into her breasts when you have finished (see *Semen*).

Breasts, vagina and clitoris all at once make the most concentrated and fastest buildup of sensation once intercourse has begun, for some women at least. Few men can

BREASTS *opposite*
Just how sensitive the breasts are, in men as well as women, varies enormously.

BREASTS *above*
Men still don't understand about breasts – or are in too much hurry to get lower down.

BUTTOCKS *opposite*
Visually, good buttocks are a turn-on almost equally for both sexes.

get a nipple orgasm, but a stiff pair of feathers is worth trying. Many easily-stimulated or well-loved women can get a rather special pleasure from suckling a baby.

She says: 'Men still don't understand about breasts, or are in too much of a hurry to get lower down – unlike a man's nipples, a woman's have a direct hot line to her clitoris. A man who can dial this correctly and will only take the time can do anything. Palm-brushing, eyelid-brushing, licking, and loud sucking like a baby can work wonders; the orgasms one gets from these are mind-blowing, without detracting a jot from intercourse to come after. *Please take time.*'

Intercourse between the breasts is equally good in other positions – head to tail, or with her on top (especially if she has small breasts), or man sitting, woman kneeling: experiment, accordingly.

buttocks

Next in line after breasts, and alternate with them as visual sex stimuli for different cultures and individuals. Actually the original primate focus, being brightly colored in most

apes: apparently equally fancied by the Mousterian culture which produced some of the best Stone Age figurines, while more recent primitives 'made their selection by ranging their women in a line and picking her out who projects furthest *a tergo*' (Darwin). Major erogenous zone in both sexes, less sensitive than breasts because they contain muscle as well as fat, and needing stronger stimulation (holding, kneading, slapping or even harder beating – see *Discipline*). Intercourse from behind is a pleasure in itself but be careful if she has a weak back. In any position the muscular movements of coitus stimulate the buttocks in both sexes, particularly if each holds the partner's rear fairly tightly, one cheek in each hand. These extra sensations are well worth cultivating deliberately. Visually, good buttocks are a turn-on almost equally for both sexes.

cassolette

French for perfume box. The natural perfume of a clean woman: her greatest sexual asset after her beauty (some would say greater than that). It comes from the whole of her – hair, skin, breasts, armpits, genitals, and the clothing she has worn: its note depends on her hair color, but no two women are the same. Men have a natural perfume too, which women are aware of, but while a man can be infatuated with a woman's personal perfume, women on the whole tend to notice if a man smells right or wrong. Wrong means not so much unpleasant as intangibly not for them. Often their awareness of a man includes conditioned extras like tobacco.

Because it is so important, a woman needs to guard her own personal perfume as carefully as her looks and learn to use it in courtship and intercourse as skillfully as she uses the rest of her body. Smoking doesn't help this. It can be a long-range weapon (nothing seduces a man more reliably, and this can happen subliminally without his knowing it) but at the same time a skillful man can read it, if he is an olfactory type, and if he knows her, to tell when she is excited.

Susceptibility and consciousness of human clean perfumes vary in both sexes. Whether these are inborn differences, like inability to smell cyanide, or whether they are due to unconscious blocking-out we don't know. Some children can't understand the point of blind man's buff because they know by smell who is touching them: some women can smell when they are pregnant. Men can't smell some chemicals related to musk unless they have a shot of female sex hormone. There is probably a whole biological signal mechanism here which we are only just starting to unravel. Far more human loves and antipathies are based on smell than our deodorant-and-aftershave culture admits. Many people, especially women, say that

CASSOLETTE *opposite*
Far more human loves and antipathies are based on smell than our soap-and-aftershave culture admits.

when it's a question of bed or not-bed they let their noses lead them.

Women have the keener sense of smell, but men respond to it more as an attractant. In lovemaking, the note changes in regular order, from the totality of skin and *gousset* to her 'excited' note, then to her full genital odor, then, when intercourse has begun, to a different scent. Finally the seminal odor will appear in her breath and trigger the next bout.

Some benighted savages still cut off the clitoris. It's said that women themselves are the most insistent about the necessity of mutilating their daughters. Ours don't go that far, but do still chop off their armpit hair, or did until a new generation started to realize that it was sexy. This might be forgiveable in a hot climate with no plumbing. Now it is simply ignorant vandalism. Some of the nicest of them still do it, and even the wouldbe sexiest are in-educable in the face of fashion. This could be played as an argument for lifeboat whiskers or Sikhism, but men's facial hair doesn't have the day-to-day importance of a woman's little tufts. These are antennae and powderpuffs to intro-duce herself in a room, or in lovemaking. They are there to brush the man's lips with; he can do the same more cir-cumspectly. Kissing deeply in the armpit leaves a partner's perfume with you. In the genital kiss, start with the lips covered, then brush the closed lips, then open her: when she gives the kiss to a man, she proceeds in the same order. It's the fullest way to become aware of her as a presence, even before you start to touch.

croupade

Any position in which he takes her squarely from behind, i.e. all rear-entry positions except those where she has one leg between his or is half-turned on her side (see *Cuissade*).

cuissade

The half-rear entry positions, where she turns her back to him and he enters with one of her legs between his and the other more or less drawn up: in some versions she lies half-turned on her side for him, still facing away.

earlobes

Underrated erogenous zone, together with the adjacent neck skin – the small area behind the ear has a 'hot line' to the visceral nerves via the vagus – and the nape of the neck. As with all extragenital sites, more effective in women than men. Once established (gentle fingering, sucking, etc., during buildup and before orgasm, to condition the response) earlobes can trigger full climax from manipula-tion alone. Some women find the noise of heavy breathing excruciating and a definite turn-off, so be careful. Heavy

CROUPADE *opposite*

earrings help, and can actually maintain subliminal erotic excitement, especially if long enough to brush the neck when she turns her head – this is the function of the large oriental and Spanish candelabra-type earrings. The sex difference in response probably accounts for their relative rarity worldwide in male fashions.

Swinging weights as erotic stimuli to condition a particular area aren't confined to the ears. If earrings are the screw-on type, take them off and try them gently on her nipples, labia or clitoris – ask first!

equipment

The Austrian gymnastic professor van Weck Erlen wrote a book in which, along with over 500 postures you draw lots to carry out, he advised a 'sexuarium' complete with gymnastic mat and trapezes. For his sort of sex you'd need

them. The idea of a 'sexuarium' complete with mirrors, re
light and black decor turns some people on – there are
good few 1930's palaces in Beverly Hills which have one
On a smaller scale one can fit out the basement. Our pre
ference is for the bedroom, however, and the resul
needn't be embarrassing.

The bed we've discussed already. The gymnastic-ma
idea isn't a bad one at all – a really thick carpet (or carpe
piece if you can't afford it wall to wall) is as good, with
plenty of room to roll around. Some people favor stool:
for the bent-over positions, front and back: as one needs
a bedroom stool, this can be chosen the right height. A
pile of hard square cushions is more suited for diversifica-
tion. Two of the bed pillows will be hard, for use in bed –
the cushions are for floor work. If you like big mirrors these
can be inside closet doors, or turn over to show a chaste
decoration. The best chair for intercourse is a fully-
upholstered one without arms. If you want to tie each other

LUISSADE *opposite*

QUIPMENT *above*
You don't need any extras to
have superlative sex, given the
right person and the right attitude.

to it, check for size and convenience – if you only want it for straight intercourse it is best padded all over: or have separate chairs for each. A ceiling mirror is fun, but expensive and obvious if you mind that. You need an adjacent bathroom and shower. The ordinary motel bedroom layout is excellent for all these things, except that they don't pick the chairs with an eye to coition.

Naturally it is exciting to set up a fantasy place for fantasy experiences, complete with your own light show, if you have the money and energy. What we don't want to do here is to give the impression that you really need this – you don't, any more than you need a dream kitchen to be a first-class chef. You need the bare minimum – privacy, heating, washing space, a bed, one or two ordinary furniture surfaces, genitalia which work, love and imagination.

If you want extras, these will depend on what you want to do. Acrobatic position-merchants like to have a

LANQUETTE *opposite*

FRONTAL *above*
All the face-to-face positions
where one partner has both
thighs between those of the other.

step-stool (fixed down, so it isn't dangerous) or even a short ladder. Some people fancy a *Rocking chair.* Old-style bordels went in for all manner of stage sets, but these were either for the obsessed or once-in-a-while settings for an extra kick, not permanencies. If you are including other couples you need corresponding extra space, whether you go all together or alternate demonstrations. Colored room light is an extra which some people find rewarding – so are a Land camera and a tape-recorder. If you use extras of any sort, from cushions or vibrators to cameras, lubri-cants, ropes or g-strings, make sure they are at hand and don't have to be fetched. Have a cloth towel ready – paper tissues stick to the skin. But you don't *need* any of these things to have superlative sex, given the right person and the right attitude.

Probably the only advantage of a really private sex-room is that you can fill it with erotic pictures without erotising 'square' guest-space, and entertain Auntie without her asking what those rings in the wall are for. But a slide projector works fine on any white wall or ceiling, and you'd be surprised how unobservant the uninitiated are.

feet

Very attractive sexually to some people—he can get an orgasm, if wished, between their soles.

Their erotic sensitivity varies a lot. Sometimes, when they're the only part you can reach, they serve as channels of communication, and the big toe is a good penis substitute (see *Big toe*).

Tickling the soles excites some people out of their minds; for others it's agony but increases general arousal. You can try it as a stimulus, or, briefly, for testing bondage. Firm pressure on the sole at the instep, however administered, is erogenic to most people. But so can almost any touch be in a woman who's that way minded – one can get a full orgasm from a foot, a finger, or an earlobe. Men respond less far but equally easily if the handling is skillful.

flanquette

The half-facing group of sexual postures – she lies facing him with one of her legs between his, and consequently one of his legs between hers, the frontal equivalent of the *Cuissades*. These positions give extra clitoral pressure from the man's thigh if he presses hard with it.

food

Dinner is a traditional preface to sex. In old-time France or Austria one booked a restaurant room with no handle on the outside of the door. At the same time there is a French saying that love and digestion went to bed together and the offspring was apoplexy. This isn't quite true. On the other hand, immediately after a heavy meal is not an ideal moment – you can easily make your partner, especially the woman if she's underneath, sick.

A meal can be an erotic experience in itself – for a demonstration of how a woman can excite a man by eating a chicken-leg or a pear 'at' him, cannibal-style, see the lovely burlesque in the film of *Tom Jones*. A meal à *deux* is, quite certainly, a direct lead-in to love play (see *Big toe*, *Remote control*) but don't overdo the alcohol, and give each other a few minutes after rising from table. Love and food mixed well in Greek and Roman times when you reclined together on a couch, or fed one another (geishas do this still). Some people enjoy food-and-sex games (custard or icecream on the skin, grapes in the pussy, and so on) which are great for regressive orality but messy for an ordinary domestic setting. Most lovers with privacy like to eat naked together and take it from there according to taste.

History is littered with 'aphrodisiac' foods – these are either magic (eryngo roots, which look like testicles, phallic asparagus and so on), olfactory (fish, tomatoes straight off the plant, which smell sexy) or miscellaneous. One can't prove that onions, eels – phallic and otherwise – ginseng root and so on don't work on some people. The trouble is that any *reputed* aphrodisiac works if you think it will, while many true pharmacological responses can get overriden in particular individuals by other factors. Broad beans are a reputed aphrodisiac – not only do they look like testicles, but they contain dopamine. We both respond so quickly to one another that any effect of this sort is hard to gauge personally. Essential oils which slightly irritate the bladder can excite some girls – try a full dose of green Chartreuse. Hot spices, which induce skin flushing, are another physiologically plausible line of attack. But none of them are lifesavers, or come up to the combined effect of 'the time and the place and the loved one together.' However, experiment by all means. Only very heavy meals and excessive drinking are specific turn-offs.

frontal

All the face-to-face positions where one partner has both thighs between those of the other – he astride both hers or between them. Includes all the varieties of the *Matrimonial* plus most of the more complicated, deep facing positions. Gives more depth (usually) but less clitoral pressure than the *Flanquettes*. To unscramble a complicated posture for purposes of classification, turn the partners round mentally and see if they can finish up face-to-face in a matrimonial without crossing legs. If so, it's frontal. If not, and they finish face-to-face astride one leg, it's a flanquette: square from behind (croupade): or from behind, astride a leg (cuissade). It's as simple as that.

This isn't an intellectual classificatory exercise. Postures are to be used in sequence, and one needs to make as few radical shifts, such as climbing over legs or turning a partner over, as possible – consider, in dancing, the difference between an impetus turn and a natural spin turn. This is important in planning sequences, though once you get used to going through five, ten or twenty postures at a single session you'll do it automatically: at first, whichever partner leads, they need to envisage all the stages in getting where they are going to avoid clumsiness and breaks, other than natural and intended ones.

FRONTAL   *overleaf*
Postures are used in sequence and one needs to make as few radical shifts as possible. Avoid clumsiness.

hair

Head hair has a lot of Freudian overtones—in mythology it's a sign of virility, witness Samson or Hercules. Our culture having learned in the last generation to associate long hair with women and short hair with manly conformity is occasionally excited to frenzy when young males now prefer to reject the stereotype and wear their hair, in the words of the seventeenth-century Harvard MS. 'in the manner of ruffians and barbarous Indians'— or of George Washington. Freud thought that long female hair acted as reassurance to the male by being a substitute for the phallus women don't have. Be that as it may, long male hair stirs all kinds of hostility in up-tight people who are upset by anything which looks intersexual in terms of their conventions. This is temporary – in many ages it has been as fashionable as now, and tends to go with a less anxious idea of maleness.

Sex play with long hair is great because of its texture – you can handle it, touch each other with it, and generally use it as one more resource. Some women are turned on by a fair amount of masculine body hair because it looks virile, others turned off by it because it looks animal – this seems to be a matter of attitude. Male face hair is another focus of convention – sometimes everyone has it as a social necessity, at other times it is persecuted, or confined to sailors, pioneers, and exotic people such as artists and chefs. Schopenhauer thought that it covered the parts of the face 'which express the moral feelings,' and disapproved, on the grounds that it was immodest to wear a sex signal in the middle of one's face. Today you can please yourself, or better, your partner.

handwork

Sex for all males and many females begins in the handwork class – both when we start to discover our own bodies and when we start to have access to each other's. For both sexes it is basic training – in mutual sex good handwork is never superseded. A couple who can masturbate each other really skillfully can do anything else they like. Handwork is not a 'substitute' for vaginal intercourse but something quite different, giving a different type of orgasm, and the orgasm one induces oneself is different again from orgasm induced by a partner. In full intercourse it is a preparation – to stiffen the man, or to give the woman one or more preliminary peaks before insertion. After intercourse, it is the natural lead-in to a further round. Moreover most men can get a second orgasm sooner from partner-stimulation than from the vagina, and a third after that if they masturbate themselves.

A woman who has the divine gift of lechery and loves her partner will masturbate him well, and a woman who knows how to masturbate a man – subtly, unhurriedly and

HAIR *opposite*
Sex play with long hair is great because of its texture – you can handle it, touch each other with it and generally use it as one more resource.

mercilessly – will almost always make a superlative partner. She needs intuitive empathy and real enjoyment of
penis, holding it in just the right place, with just the right
amount of pressure and movement, and timing her action
in bursts to coincide with his feeling – stopping or slowing
to keep him in suspense, speeding up to control his climax.
Some men can't stand really proficient masturbation to
climax unless they are securely tied (see *Bondage*), and
virtually none can hold still for slow masturbation.

The variation can be endless, even if she hasn't the
choice of foreskin back, foreskin not back, which again
yield two quite distinct nuances. If he isn't circumcised
she will probably need to avoid rubbing the glans itself
except in pursuit of very special effects. Her best grip is
just below the groove, with the skin back as far as it will
go, and using two hands – one pressing hard near the
root, holding the penis steady, or fondling the scrotum,
the other making a thumb-and-first finger ring, or a whole-
hand grip. She should vary this, and, in prolonged masturbation, change hands often. For a full orgasm she sits comfortably on his chest or kneels astride him. During every
extended sexual session one orgasm – usually the second
or third – is well worth giving in this way: the French pro-
fessionals who used no other method and called themselves 'les filles de la veuve Poignet' didn't only stay in
business through fear of infection. It is well worth devoting
time to perfecting this technique – it fully expresses love,
and can be domesticated in any bedroom. Rolling the
penis like pastry between the palms of two hands is
another technique, best used for producing an erection.
Firm pressure with one finger at the midpoint between
penis and anus is another. For some occasions she can try
to copy his own favorite method of self-masturbation;
using her own rhythm has a different and sometimes more
startling effect.

He needs to notice how she masturbates herself. Most
men neglect the labia in favor of the clitoris. Clitoral rubbing can be as mind-blowing for her as slow masturbation
is for him, but it can be painful if it is unskillful, repeated too
often or straight after an orgasm achieved in this way. She
says: 'The main difficulty from the man's point of view is
that the ideal pressure point varies from hour to hour·so
he should allow her to guide him to the right place. Most
men think they know automatically, having succeeded
once – they are often wrong.'

For preparation as well as orgasm, the flat of the hand
on the vulva with the middle finger between the lips, and
its tip moving in and out of the vagina, while the ball of the
palm presses hard just above the pubis, is probably the
best method. Steady rhythm is the most important thing,
taking it from her hip movements, and alternating with

gentle lip stretching – then a full attack on the clitoris and its hood with the forefinger or little finger, thumb deeply in the vagina (keep your nails short). For faster response, hold her open with one hand and work gently with all the fingers of the other (in this case she may need to be fixed down). Switch to the tongue occasionally if she becomes dry, because she won't realize until afterwards how sore you have made her.

In mutual masturbation to orgasm you take out your need to move on your partner. It works better than sixty-nine because under these circumstances you can let go without losing your partner or hurting them. Side by side on your backs is probably the best position.

When she masturbates him, she may get extra pleasure from seeing his ejaculation – if you want to avoid spilling semen in a strange bed, use one of the short glans-condoms called American tips (this is their only use – they are dangerous contraceptives, as they come off during intercourse).

However much sex you have, you will still need simple, own-hand masturbation – not only during periods of separation, but simply when you feel like another orgasm. Some women feel left out if they find their partner mastur-

HANDWORK *opposite and above*
In mutual sex good handwork is never superseded.

bating; but if you feel vibrations when he thinks you are asleep and want to get in on the act, tackle him there and then and finish him yourself at full speed – or better, start on him slow-style then stop, tie him, and make him watch you masturbate yourself, slowly and with style, before you put him out of his misery. The unexpected sight of a woman giving herself an orgasm when he cannot move is unbearably exciting for most men. Make sure he can't get loose. Finally, watching each other take the last orgasm separately but together makes a wonderful end to any afternoon in bed.

kisses

These, at one level, don't require teaching, but it's easy to be so set on insertion that one overlooks them. (See *Real sex*). Lip and tongue kisses add immensely to intercourse in all face-to-face positions: breast kisses are essential if the woman isn't to miss a whole range of feeling; genital kisses (see *Mouth music*) are a tender resource on their own. Kisses can be put anywhere on the body, they can be given with lips, tongue, penis, labia or eyelashes – mouth kisses range from a mere touch to the kiss *à la cannibale* which leaves a bruise.

A lot of people maintain mouth contact continuously throughout intercourse, and prefer face-to-face positions for this reason. The deep tongue kiss can either be a second penetration, the man's tongue imitating exactly the rhythm of what is going on elsewhere, or she can give it, penetrating him, to call the rhythm. Even without any penetration, some people favor a tongue-battle which can last minutes or hours, with several orgasms for the girl, a form of non-genital heavy petting called *maraichignage*. If you are in private, move on to breasts, and go from there. Another pleasure is to make her a carpet of flowers, by covering every inch of her body with small, close kisses: then she can reply, using lipstick to mark where she's been. From there it is only a little way to doing the same with a tongue-tip (see *Tongue bath*): moreover, unlike a man, she has two mouths to kiss with, and some women use them beautifully. Eyelids too can be used for nipple, lip, glans and skin kisses.

If you haven't at least kissed her mouth, shoulders, neck, breasts, armpits, fingers, palms, toes, soles, navel, genitals and earlobes, you haven't really kissed her: it is no trouble to fill in the gaps for completeness and makes a touching compliment.

A good mouth kiss should leave its recipient breathless but not asphyxiated (leave an airway open), and nobody likes their nose squashed into their face. Clean your teeth before making love, and if you are having whisky, garlic, etc., both of you have it.

HANDWORK *opposite*
A woman with the divine gift of lechery will almost always make a superlative partner.

KISSES *overleaf*
Make her a carpet of flowers by covering every inch of her body with small, close kisses.

little death

Le petite mort: some women do indeed pass right out, the 'little death' of French poetry. Men occasionally do the same. The experience is not unpleasant, but it can scare an inexperienced partner cold. A friend of ours had this happen with the first girl he ever slept with. On recover she explained, 'I'm awfully sorry, but I always do that.' By then he had called the police and the ambulance. So there is no cause for alarm, any more than over the yells, convulsions, hysterical laughter or sobbing, or any of the other quite unexpected reactions which go with complete orgasm in some people. By contrast others simply shut their eyes, but enjoy it no less. Sound and fury can be a flattering testimonial to a partner's skills, but a fallacious one, because they don't depend on the intensity of feeling, nor it upon them.

Men don't very often pass right out – that's *her* privilege, though they can give a splendid impersonation of a fit. In any case you'll soon get to know your partner's pattern.

lubrication

The best sexual lubricant is saliva. Except for anal intercourse, most greasy materials such as petroleum jelly are too greasy and being unwettable they leave an unpleasant feel. Jellies tend to cut sensation too much. The normal excited vagina is correctly set for friction; if she is too wet, as may happen on the Pill, dry gently with a handkerchief-wrapped finger (not tissues – you'll never stop finding the bits). To increase friction, try honey – it washes off easily and is harmless.

Interference with friction is the main drawback of contraceptive creams, foams and so on, making them unpopular with some couples.

matrimonial

MATRIMONIAL
opposite and overleaf
The good old Adam and Eve missionary position.

Every culture has its own fads about best positions, and experiment is essential. If we come back to the good old Adam and Eve missionary position, with him on top, astride or between, and her underneath facing – and we do come back to it – that is because it's uniquely satisfying. Chiefly it's unique in its adaptability to mood; it can be wildly tough or very tender, long or quick, deep or shallow. It is the starting point for nearly every sequence, second only to the side positions, and the most reliably mutual finishing-point for orgasm. If you start in it you can deepen it by raising her legs, move to the clitoris by putting one leg between hers, roll about or right over finishing with her on top, kneel and lie back into the Letter X with each partner lying between the other's legs (see *X position*), move into back, side or standing positions, then come back for the finish. It is also, together with the deeper versions, the ideal quick-orgasm position for both sexes. The only equally quick position for him is from behind if she is very tight, and the only quicker for her is astride on top. In fact, the chief reason for using the other 600 positions is to delay his final orgasm while multiplying hers. Experimentation will show you which suit you best.

Even excluding the leg-raising variants this position has won more medals at international expositions than any other. On the other hand, there is no one surefire sex

position which suits everyone. There are nonfrigid women who never come in this position, or only rarely: whether this is due to unconscious forces or position of the vulva, which can be a problem, doesn't matter a damn – try another position, especially if the man is overweight. The matrimonial and all deep or weightbearing positions are now known to be a bad idea in pregnancy: a few non-pregnant non-responders have had their lives changed by one or two hard pillows under the buttocks. There are non-matrimoniable women who have to be taken sitting, face to face, or from behind, finger to clitoris, or who need to ride. If the man needs her flat to finish, give her several orgasms in her preferred position first, then turn her. A gentleman is defined as one who takes his weight on his hands. There are great advantages anyway in ending in a position where you can settle in each other's arms without exertion.

The tuning adjustments for matrimonials can be highly important – hard enough bed, use of pillows if she is slim or built that way. Bed, cushion and flesh should between them give the consistency of buttocks which would be esthetically a bit too big. Tough or tender, how high you ride, pinned down (fold her arms gently up behind her and hold each of her thumbs in one of your hands) or not pinned down, astride her legs (holding them open by putting a foot under each of her insteps) or between them, spreading her with your legs – all make subtle differences. If your pubis isn't very hard and she needs a touch more clitoris, try a leg-between position or add finger contact. She can for her part hold your foreskin or penile shaft skin forcibly back with her hand (see *Florentine*).

menstruation

Primitives avoid menstrual intercourse because it is bad magic, and many moderns because it is messy. At the same time, the height of a period may be the girl's randiest time. If so, intercourse is harmless unless the male is liable to attacks of urethritis. You can ignore the flow and wash after, or she can douche, put in a cap, and flush afterwards (this is inclined to make her too dry, however). But periods are the natural time to concentrate on learning the full, mutual use of other, replacement techniques. Nature programmed them to encourage your versatility. Shallow, labial penetration is effective with a tampon in place – or you can try having sex under a running shower instead of in bed. The magical hazards can now be discounted, whatever grandmother taught. Try pretending that her g-string is a locked chastity belt and see how many ways, orgasm-wise, you can circumvent it. See *Substitutes*.

missionary position

Name given by amused Polynesians, who preferred squatting intercourse, to the European matrimonial. Libel on one of the most rewarding sex positions.

mons pubis

The decorative fat-pad over the female pubic bone which acts as a buffer in face-to-face intercourse and (more important) serves to transmit sensation to the rest of the area when it moves. Many men are not aware, if they are oversold on direct clitoris stimulation, that most women can be brought to orgasm simply by holding this gently in

MISSIONARY POSITION   *above*

the cupped hand and kneading or shaking it, before, without, or as well as putting a finger in the vulva (see *Pubic hair*). You can either grasp it (it exactly fits the palm) or rest the heel of your hand on it while using the fingers on the labia, or you can cup the whole area, mons and closed labia, in your palm and fingers. Practice seeing how much sensation you can produce with your partner lying completely closed.

mouth music

It wasn't many years ago that genital kisses, or rather the taboos on them, were a king pretext for divorce on grounds of perversity, cruelty and so on. We've come some way since then – now there are textbooks, and they figure in movies. Personal preferences and unpreferences apart, most people now know that they are one of the best things in sexual intimacy.

Mutuality is the order of the day, which is why marriage manuals stress soixante-neuf. This is fine, but is has a few practical drawbacks. The chief is that this sort of lovemaking belongs better to the playing-the-instrument category than to the completely mutual. It needs attention and care to give your partner your best, and consequently you can't go beserk over it, as you can over a mutual genital orgasm: impending orgasm, especially in the woman, just isn't compatible with careful technique, and the man can even be bitten. Another slight, but in some men, real defect is that in soixante-neuf the woman is the wrong way around for tongue work on the most sensitive surface of the glans (this explains the acrobatics in some Indian temple statues, which aim to get both mutuality and a better approach for the woman). Our own experience is that mutual genital kisses are wonderful, but if you are going to orgasm it's usually better to take turns.

Who goes first is clearly a matter of preference, but one can give the woman dozens of purely preliminary orgasms in this way, as many as she can take, and she will still want to go on from there, so the man had better save himself for later. A few men can't take even the shortest genital kiss before ejaculating – these should save it until they need a new erection, when it is a uniquely effective way of raising the dead.

Some girls do and some don't like the man to go all the way and ejaculate (if they love him very much, that may make all the difference, but not always). Those who don't can easily stop just short of getting him there, shift to another *foyer* (between the breasts, for example) or they can compress with both hands to gain time – this needs alertness and doesn't always work. It's also apt to wreck his orgasm. Others once they are used to it don't

find the experience complete unless their lover does
ejaculate. John Hunter wrote, 'The semen would appear
both by smell and taste to be a mawkish kind of substance:
but when held in the mouth it produced a warmth similar
to spices.' If the slight bitterness, rather than the whole
idea, is what they dislike, it can easily be avoided by taking
him really deeply. With experienced women we guess it is
about fifty-fifty, come or not come; in any case you can
always ask, and partners soon learn each others' tastes.
She says: 'A couple of important points to remember here
are the retching is a reflex action if something large is
poked down your throat; so if she does retch it may well
not be because she hates it but because she can't help
herself. A large penis will also stretch the mouth quite a
lot and if she is covering her teeth with her lips to protect
you, violent movements may lacerate them. Be considerate.'

Normal genital odor is a big part of the genital kiss
for both partners, which means that the parties should
wash often, but not immediately beforehand: they ought
to know each other well enough to say, if it is ever
disagreeable, and switch or wait. A few minutes' vigorous
intercourse will often put this right, though the woman's
odor changes in character. Contraceptives can upset it
too. The marketers of intimate deodorants and flavored
vaginal douches show evidence only of sexual inexperience – nobody wants peach sauce on, say, scampi.
Seaweed odors or musk would be more in key. The
woman's *Cassolette* is her secret weapon to an extent
that women in America don't seem to realize–French
women know better. Some men respond violently to it
without realizing the fact; it's also the ideal perfume
fixative, and a touch behind the ears at a dance, in advance
of, or instead of, bottle perfume can be deadly. His, by
contrast, will please her more the longer she loves him.
Wash with white soap, and here as everywhere treat
deodorants the way a chef would treat deflavorants. How
the hippie generation thinks you can live the good sex
life without washing defeats explanation.

For some couples the simultaneous, 69-type kiss
really does represent the ultimate in sensation. For them,
since loss of control will be complete, the woman can't be
the beserk type, nor want him to stop short of ejaculating.
The woman-on-top position in most books is all right,
especially if she combines mouth with handwork, but it
gives the man a stiff neck. We favor the no-cushions
position, i.e. head to tail on their sides, each with the under
thigh drawn up as a cushion for the partner's head. The
man can open her widely by slipping his arm in the crook
of her upper knee.

The mutual kiss can be long or short; the short is just

in passing – the long can last minutes or hours according to taste and speed. Both fit nicely between rounds of intercourse, as well as acting as hors d'oeuvres or a corpse reviver.

If, on the other hand, they are going alternately, let him start, preferably in this same no-cushions position, while she does very little. Then it can be her turn; or they can go on to intercourse, putting off fellatio until he has had one orgasm and a rest and is due for his next erection. In this way she can abandon herself, and watch her technique when she sucks him. She will probably get the best results with what the Chinese call the 'jade flute' position – an instrument which is self-explanatory, and is played like a recorder, facing him, thumbs underneath, fingers on top. Her technique depends on her man – for instance, on whether or not he is circumcised. Not all men find tongue or lip contact with the glans pleasurable. For some it's ecstasy, while others prefer foreskin movement over the covered glans with the shaft held tight. The various sorts of nibbling, etc., described in sex books come naturally to most people. One finds them out on a basis of learn and teach. For a more active male position and a fast orgasm, she lies back, and he has oral coitus as fully and deeply as she can stand it. She must keep her teeth well open, making him a vagina with her lips and tongue. He needs to keep a little control, to avoid being involuntarily bitten.

The reverse equivalent is when she kneels astride and gives herself, exactly as in a passionate mouth-to-mouth kiss, brushing first, then open and deeply, while he uses long tongue strokes, from the vagina to the clitoris, with an extra twitch to her glans as he reaches it each time.

When it's his initiative, he can do worse than try the cascade position, if she is portable. This is really only 69 standing up, but it gives her the unique sensation of an orgasm head-downward. To get her there he lays her face-up across the bed, head over the edge, stands astride her face, then bends over and picks her up, legs round his neck. She can return his kiss, but near orgasm she had far better slip him between her breasts or into her hand, and abandon herself to full orgasm.

The first genital kiss, to an inexperienced girl, is another 'situation.' Kneeling before her, 'vers le buisson ardent des femmes' looks fine, but one can't reach to do more than nuzzle. We suggest this: with the lady face-up along the bed, sit on the edge half-facing her feet. Kiss her all over; then reach over and pick up her farther leg and kiss her foot. Quickly slip your nearer elbow through her raised knee, open her, and kiss gently on the closed labia until she is ready for deeper and deeper tongue strokes. Fewer and fewer women are now inhibited about being kissed, though rather more can't get pleasure from kissing the man. A surprising number of girls cannot initially be got there at all *without* prolonged genital kissing, a fact which Indian love books recognize. For a very shy girl (or man), try it in the dark – but certainly try it. In the other direction, good mouth work is perhaps one of the most valued gifts a girl can give to her man, and well worth practicing. A spontaneous genital kiss to a man is one of the most moving gestures in the whole sexual experience.

navel

Fascinating to lovers, like all the details of the human body. It's not only decorative but has a lot of cultivable sexual sensation; it fits the finger, tongue, glans or big toe, and merits careful attention when you kiss or touch. Intercourse in the navel is practicable (there are stories of naive couples who thought that was the usual way, and it's a common childhood fantasy about how sex is conducted). If she is plump she can hold up the skin on each side to make labia. In any case, the finger or tongue tip slip into it naturally in both sexes.

négresse

A la Négresse – from behind. She kneels, hands clasped behind her neck, breasts and face on the bed. He kneels behind – she hooks her legs over his and pulls him to her with them – he puts a hand on each of her shoulder-blades and presses down. Very deep position – apt to pump her full of air which escapes later in a disconcerting manner – otherwise excellent.

postures

Endless. time has been spent throughout history, chiefly by nonplaying coaches, in describing and giving fancy names to upwards of six hundred of these – collecting them is obviously a human classificatory hobby. Most people now know the obvious ones and have learned which make for quick and slow orgasm and how to use them in series. A few people, either for symbolic or anatomical reasons, can only get orgasm in one or two.

We haven't gone into postures here in this kind of detail. Most of the non-freak ones come naturally, and few of the freak postures merit more than a single visit out of curiosity.

The only part we regret is the loss of the fancy names, Arabic, Sanskrit or Chinese, which go with them. Inspection will indicate which fit special situations such as pregnancy, fat male with thin girl, height differences, etc.

NAVEL *opposite*
The finger and the tongue tip slip into it naturally.

POSTURES *overleaf*
Only trial will indicate which work best, or at all.

Only trial will indicate which work best, or at all, orgasm wise. Couples often start by trying the lot, but nearly inevitably end up with one or two, going back to the book for special occasions. Some of the really wild fantasies in Oriental manuscripts do have a point – the girl astride in Mughal pictures who is balancing lighted lamps on her hands, head and shoulders or shooting at a target with a bow is only showing that she can bring the man off with her vaginal muscles alone while keeping the rest of her still (see *Pompoir*) and so on. Others are mystical or merely gymnastic. All the poses we show are practicable (we've tried them for fit, if not to orgasm) and more or less rewarding.

quickies

Short and sharp has a charm of its own, but it needs a rate of mutual turn-on and physical response in the woman which is learned as a rule *only* in much longer sessions. A really good couple can manage either at will – short and sweet, or indefinitely prolonged and differently sweet. In other words you can't fully appreciate the quickie without mastering the art of prolongation.

Once you've got this, the quickie is the equivalent of inspiration, and you should let it strike lightning fashion, any time and almost anywhere, from bed in the middle of the night to halfway up a spiral stair: anywhere that you're suddenly alone and the inspiration is bilateral. Not that one of other won't sometimes specifically ask, but the inspirational quickie is mutual, and half the fun is that the preliminary communication is wordless between real lovers. The rule is never to resist this linkup if it's at all possible – with quickness, wit and skill it usually is. This means proficiency in handling sitting, standing and other postures, and making love without undressing. The ideal quickie position, the nude matrimonial, will often be out. This may mean on a chair, against a tree, in a washroom. If you have to wait and can go straight home, it will keep up to half an hour. Longer than that and it's a new occasion. Around the house, try not to block, even if you *are* busy.

rear entry

The other human option – for most mammals it's the only one. Works admirably standing, lying, kneeling, sitting, or with the woman astride. The lack of face-to-faceness is

CKIES *opposite*
u should let it strike lightning
hion, any time and almost
ywhere, from bed to half way
a spiral stair.

R ENTRY *below*
orks admirably standing, lying,
eeling, sitting or with the
man astride.

more than compensated for by extra depth and buttock stimulation, hand access to breasts and clitoris, and the sight of a pretty rear view. For the standing positions she needs something of the right height to support her – in the head-down kneeling positions you need to be careful

not to push her face into the mattress, and in all of the deep variants you need to avoid going too deep too hard, or you will hit an ovary, which is as painful as hitting a testicle. A few women are put off by the symbolism – 'doing it like animals,' 'not being valued if we aren't face to face' – but the physical payoff is so intense that they shouldn't allow these feelings to make them miss it. They could try it first with the man lying on his back and the girl lying faceup on top of him, or kneeling astride facing away, though these don't give the unique depth and total perineal stimulation of the rear kneeling positions (see *Négresse*). The man can hold her breasts or pubis, or, if she likes to be controlled, grasp her wrists behind her. A pile of hard pillows under her middle will help to prevent the position collapsing if she doesn't like being forcibly held, or she can kneel on the floor with her chest on the bed or a chair-seat. The head-down position is best for depth and total apposition – avoid it if it hurts her, or if she has a weak back, or if she is pregnant. Some women like a finger on the clitoris during intercourse, and this is easy in all rear positions. It's worth trying in any case, as it totally alters the range of sensation. Grasping the whole pussy in one hand gives a different sensation again and doesn't give the excessive sharpness which comes from strong clitoral stimulation. Or you can withdraw briefly and give a few clitoral strokes with the glans, guiding it with your hand.

While the deep kneeling position is, or can be, one of the toughest, from behind on your sides is about the gentlest (*à la paresseuse* – the lazy position) and can even be done in sleep – best if she draws her top thigh up a little and sticks her bottom out. This is one position which, in many women, can be managed with very little or even no erection; it can help to cure partial impotence or nervousness on the male side by restoring morale. It's also excellent if you want it gentle for health reasons, for fat or slightly disabled people, and so on.

It's well worth experimenting with the full range of rear positions at least as fully as with the face-to-face series, because there will be at least one you'll almost certainly use regularly along with the matrimonial and its variants and the woman-astride positions.

scrotum

Basically, a control device to keep the testes at the right temperature for sperm production – moves up when you are cold and down when you are warm. It is also a highly sensitive skin area, but needs careful handling, since pressure on a testis is highly painful to its proprietor. Gentle tongue and finger work or cupping in the hand is about right. You can take it right into your mouth.

AR ENTRY *above*
s well worth experimenting with
e whole range of rear positions.

showerbath

Natural venue for sexual adventures – wash togethe
make love together: only convenient overhead point i
most apartments or hotel rooms to attach a partner'
hands. Don't pull down the fixture, however – it isn'
weightbearing. See *Discipline*.

skin

Skin is our chief extragenital sexual organ – grossly unde
rated by most men, who tend to concentrate on the peni
and clitoris; better understood by women.

She says: 'The smell and feel of a man's skin probabl
has more to do with sexual attraction (or the opposite

opposite
chief extragenital sexual
⬛n – grossly underrated by
⬛ men.

than any other single feature, even though you may not be conscious of it.'

Skin stimulation is a major component of all sex. Not only its feel when touched, but its coolness, texture and tightness are triggers for a whole range of sex feelings. These can be boosted in some people by emphasis, and by adding other textures, especially fur, rubber, leather or tight clothing. Much underrated part of human sexual response, to be played to the full if it turns you on. See *Clothes, Friction rub, Pattes d'araignée, Tongue bath*. Use these to educate your own and your partner's skin.

ding positions

The traditional 'upright' is a quickie, and apt to produce stiff male muscles unless she is tall. Many women need to stand on two Manhattan phone directories with the yellow pages, or an equivalent. Best undertaken up against a solid object such as a wall or a tree (not a door, whichever way it opens). Alternatively, you can be free standing, legs apart for stability and arms clasped round each other's buttocks – looking down as you move can be really sensual.

There are two kinds of positions – this one, subject to a good match in height, and the Hindu versions where he picks her up: these are tremendous if she is light as an Oriya dancing girl, otherwise they need to be executed in water to make her weightless (see *Bathing*). For a tall girl, try with her arms round your neck, one of her feet on the ground, and the other over your elbow. She can then go legs around waist, both legs over your arms, and even both legs round your neck, lying back, if you are strong enough, into a head-down position. Try this over a bed in case you drop her, but stand on a firm floor, not a mattress. If you are back up to a wall she can swing herself with one foot. Not good orgasm positions – designed rather to spin out coition. Standing positions from behind need no special comment – she needs to lean over or hold onto something rigid. If you have real height problems, try the upright positions on a flight of stairs. The head-down genital kiss is a winner if you are strong enough to hold her up, and she takes a good leg grip.

tongue bath

Going systematically over every square inch of a partner, tied if they like, with long, slow, broad tongue strokes. Start behind, turn them and cover the front surface after, so as to be in position to go on to coition or hand and mouth work. If the woman gives this, she follows it by covering the whole available surface equally systematically with slow strokes of her open vulva. Mini-versions cover particular areas in the same way.

upper hands

If the matrimonial is the king of postures, the queen is her turn on top, 'riding St. George.' Indian erotology is the only ancient tradition devoid of stupid patriarchal hangups about the need for her to be underneath, and unashamed about accepting her fully aggressive role in reciprocal sex. With a woman who has good vaginal muscle control it can be fantastic for the man, but for her it is unique, giving her total freedom to control movement, depth and her partner. She can lean forward for breast or

ANDING POSITIONS
ove and opposite
aditional upright is apt to
roduce stiff male muscles unless
e is tall.

UPPER HANDS *above*
Riding St. George.

X POSITION *opposite*
A winner for prolonged slow
intercourse.

mouth kisses, back to show herself to him, touch her own
clitoris as she moves, delay if she wishes, for emphasis –
the lot. She can also ride him facing or facing away, or turn
from one into the other, once or often. Riding postures
need a stiff erection (or she may bend him painfully with

an over-hurried insertion). This is about the only kind of intercourse in which one or both can be injured by clumsiness or by slipping, so test yourselves gradually. Once in, she can go facing, backing, kneeling, sitting, crosslegged upon him. sideways or round and round, and make movements in three dimensions and circularly with her hips. She can also lie on him (reversed matrimonial), legs astride or between. When she has taken her main orgasm he can either turn her, or she can lie back astride him, head between his feet, without disconnecting, and go on in the letter X or the full matrimonial for his orgasm. Since it needs a stiff erection, and some women prefer to start from foreplay laterally or underneath, this makes a good second-figure of a series. If she wants to bring him to orgasm this way they should try it first, preferably on waking and when he is fresh, with a hard waking erection The round-and-round and cinder-sifting motions of the woman's hips – what the French call the Lyons mail-coach (*la diligence de Lyon*) – come easily with practice if you've got the right personality.

x position

A winner for prolonged slow intercourse. Start with her sitting facing astride him, penis fully inserted. She then lies right back until each partner's head and trunk are between the other's wide-open legs, and they clasp hands. Slow, coordinated wriggling movements will keep him erect and her close to orgasm for long periods. To switch back to other positions, either of them can sit up without disconnecting.

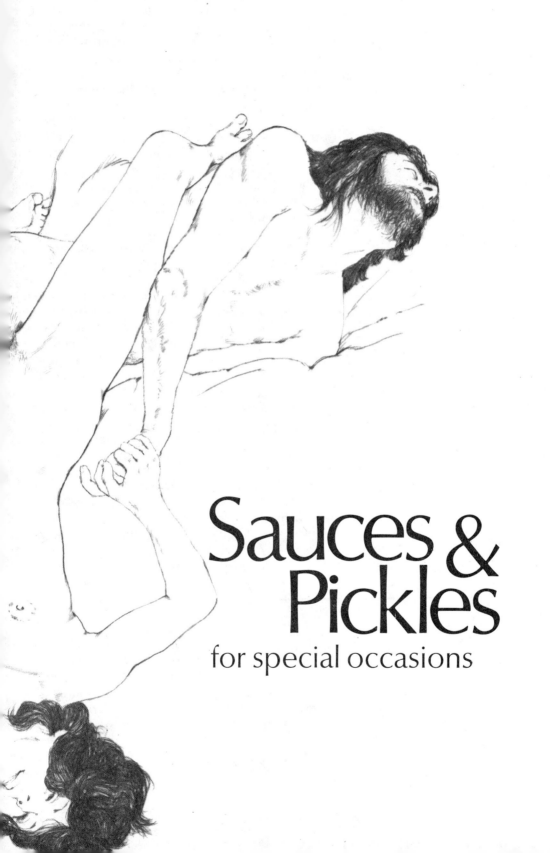

Sauces & Pickles

for special occasions

anal intercourse

This is something which nearly every couple tries once. A few stay with it, usually because the woman finds that it gives her intenser feelings than the normal route and it is pleasantly tight for the man. In England and in some states of the United States it is actually illegal.

Unlike almost any other common sex practice, this one does have drawbacks. Usually the first try is painful, and while this may go with practice it certainly won't if you have hemorrhoids; it *can* cause injury, as the area wasn't designed for that, and extreme gentleness on the man's part is needed – anal rape, even of a willing victim, is accordingly out. Also, if you use it, don't mix it with straight vaginal intercourse – this leads to troublesome infections in some people with yeasts and other organisms which belong in the gut, not the vagina or the male urethra.

On the other hand, there are lovers who vastly enjoy it, as an occasional, or even as a regular, method, and, as we said, nearly everyone, if honest, would probably be curious to try it once. The technique is quite different from ordinary penetration. With the woman kneeling, head well down, carefully lubricate your glans (this needs oil or vaseline – saliva isn't enough). *Don't*, as in ordinary insertion, make a joyous virile thrust. Put the glans to the spot and press gently and steadily, while she 'bears down' to let you in. At first she will close up tight. Then after a few moments she will begin to open. Go in slowly, never more than glans-deep, and take your friction on the pull rather than the push. Work on her breasts and clitoris meanwhile.

You can use a small vibrator or a greased finger anally during ordinary face-to-face intercourse, in men, women or both (see *Postillionage*) – this, with the little finger, is a great favorite in French sex books. The anus is sensitive in most people, and the sensitivity can be cultivated. Unless you find it very rewarding and are free from the feeling that it's inesthetic, we doubt if it's worth doing more than satisfying curiosity and the occasional impulse this way, however.

armpit

Classical site for kisses. Should on no account be shaved (see *Cassolette*). Can be used instead of the palm to silence your partner at climax – if you use your palm, rub it over your own and your partner's armpit area first.

Axillary intercourse is an occasional variation. Handle it as for intermammary intercourse (see *Breasts*) but with your penis under her right arm – well under, so that friction is on the shaft, not the glans, as in any other unlubricated area. Put her left arm round your neck and hold her right hand behind her with your right hand. She will get her sensations from the pressure against her breasts, helped by your big toe pressed to her clitoris if she wants it. Not an outstandingly rewarding trick but worth trying if you like the idea.

bathing

Bathing together is a natural concomitant of sex and a splendid overture or tailpiece. Taking an ordinary bath together has a charm of its own, though someone has to lean against the plumbing. Soaping one another all over, and, of course, drying one another, is a 'skin game' which leads on naturally to better things; after intercourse, a bath together is a natural come-back to domesticity or work. There are now large baths and conversation baths, but most of us see them only in expense account hotels.

Actual coitus is possible, and fun, in the shower if your heights match (see *Showerbath*) but no ordinary domestic or hotel bath is big enough for intercourse without punishing your elbows. Beside the novelty there isn't too much point anyway.

Sex while bathing is a different matter. The whole idea of intercourse in water is that it's like weightlessness or flying – the girl who is too big for all those Hindu climbing and standing postures becomes light enough to handle, and one can prop her at angles no acrobat could hold. All this has been rediscovered in the California swimming-

ARMPIT *above*
Classical site for kisses.

pool era; when we get to the design of the future, indoor equivalents will certainly spread among non-millionaires. Meanwhile there is the sea, after dark, when it is warm enough – on a gradually shelving beach one can have enough privacy even by day, and even re-emerge clothed: spectators will take it for callisthenics or life-saving. A pool has extras like steps and handholds, but is usually chlorinated. Water doesn't hinder friction, though its relative chill may mean that it takes some brisk rubbing to get an erection even in a very eager male. It might be a good idea to insert before going in, if possible, or for the girl to wear a diaphragm – we haven't heard of any harm coming from being pumped full of seawater, but chlorinated pool water might just possibly be irritant, as it is to the eyes. You can have excellent straight intercourse lying in the surf if you can get a beach to yourselves, but sand is a problem, and keeps appearing for days afterwards. A floating mattress is effectively a waterbed, but it is hard to stay on it without concentrating. We've heard of people combining coitus with swimming, and even scuba-diving, but they gave no practical details. Underwater coition, if more than a token contact, would use up vast amounts of air because of the overbreathing which goes with orgasm.

big toe

The pad of the male big toe applied to the clitoris or the vulva generally is a magnificent erotic instrument. The famous gentleman in erotic prints who is keeping six women occupied is using tongue, penis, both hands and both big toes. Use the toe in mammary or armpit intercourse or any time you are astride her, or sit facing as she lies or sits. Make sure the nail isn't sharp. In a restaurant, in these days of tights, one can surreptitiously remove a shoe and sock, reach over, and keep her in almost continuous orgasm with all four hands fully in view on the table top and no sign of contact – a party-trick which rates as really advanced sex. She has less scope, but can learn to masturbate him with her two big toes. The toes are definitely erogenic areas, and can be kissed, sucked, tickled, or tied with stimulating results.

bites

Hindu eroticians classified these at huge length. Gentle nibbling (of the penis, breasts, skin, fingers, ears, labia, clitoris, armpit hair) is part of the general excitatory repertoire. Hard bites at the moment of orgasm excite some people, but for most, like other painful stimuli, they are a turn-off. Women tend to bite more often than men, perhaps because they enjoy being bitten more than men do. (Remember that often your partner will do to you what they really want done to them – being aware of this is the great secret of communicating sex.) Love-bruises, on the neck and elsewhere, which some lovers find act like a constant playback, setting off more lovemaking every time they are seen, aren't made by biting but by strong, continuous suction kisses. Sharp nips to the skin aren't as a rule erotic.

Be careful of biting at or near orgasm – the jaws go into spasm and you can bite really hard – in fact don't have an orgasm deliberately with a breast, penis or finger in your mouth. The need to bite can be taken out on something neutral like cloth or hair. This seems to be a case where the mammalian program of reflexes is over-tough for human enjoyment.

blowing

Not the slang sense (see *Mouth music*) but quite simply making a current of air on the (preferably pre-wetted) skin of any part of the body, either from the lips or from a hair-drier with the heat turned off. The best way to moisten an erogenous area is with the tongue, though for more extensive operations one can obviously use water or lotion. Air on a wet sensitive surface produces a sensation which can drive some people of either sex out of their minds – experiment on a small scale, using your natural equipment (saliva and breath). In the case of earlobes, breathe in, not out, or you'll deafen your partner. Elsewhere use steady continuous exhalation with the lips about an inch from the skin. The natural sequel to a tongue bath. For a bigger operation, use the hairdrier – the result is far wilder than the conventional routine with feathers, except for palms and soles – try mixing the two by hitching a couple of feathers to the drier nozzle on threads. Never (see *Hazards*) use a strong air source, and never blow into the vagina or any other body orifice (except the mouth – but mouth-to-mouth resuscitation isn't particularly erogenous).

bondage

Bondage, or as the French call it, ligottage, is the gentle art of tying up your sex partner – not to overcome reluctance but to boost orgasm. It's one unscheduled sex technique which a lot of people find extremely exciting but are scared to try, and a venerable human resource for increasing sexual feeling, partly because it's a harmless expression of sexual aggression – something we badly need, our culture being very up-tight about it – and still more because of its physical effects: a slow orgasm when unable to move is a mind-blowing experience for anyone not too frightened of their own aggressive self to try it.

Any restraint upon muscular and emotional activity

BATHING *above*
Taking an ordinary bath together has a charm of its own, though someone has to lean against the plumbing.

generally,' wrote Havelock Ellis, 'tends to heighten the state of sexual excitement.' Men and women have always been excited anyhow by the idea of getting the better of each other, and 'erotic bondage' was always a popular turn-on – every self-respecting folk-heroine and most folk-heroes have to be bound hand and foot periodically so they can be rescued. The best man at a Berber wedding ties up the bride if she struggles, and she is expected to struggle so she can be tied up. Fantasies of the same sort have a big written and pornopicture literature (most of it wildly unpracticable and meant to be seen not felt) which act as a substitute for people who are hung up on aggression, or need an illusion of rape to be able to lie back and enjoy without guilt. Most of us have traces of these needs, and like to 'dominate' each other symbolically at times, or be dominated (no offence to Women's Lib, because this need is mutual). But bondage games are played by many straight lovers who want kicks, not substitutes, and fill a lot of important spaces. They take a little learning (first efforts are often painful, or come adrift, or waste an erection messing around) but with speed and skill many unlikely people swear by them as an occasional – if only because really professional slow masturbation isn't possible unless the subject is securely tied.

In fact, really skillful bondage works like a bomb, sexually, on most non-timid males, both on the giving. and the receiving end (as with any trick which involves both stimulation and symbolism, a well-tied sexual 'prisoner' both looks and feels sexy) – and on a fair proportion of girls once they get the idea; eventual responders of both sexes can require a lot of gentle preparation if they are scared by the aggressive symbolism, but this kind of fantasy only frightens people whose idea of tenderness is over-tender. Some women sense the need to be 'overpowered' sometimes. Others dig the domination symbol and like to be aggressors from the start. The idea is to tie your partner hand and foot, firmly but comfortably, so that they can struggle as hard as they like without getting loose, and then bring them to orgasm. Apart from being a wild sexual sensation, it enables many people who can't otherwise do so to let go to the last degree. They may yell blue murder at the critical moment but love it (one important skill here is to distinguish the noises which mean real distress – kinked wrists, cramp or the like – from the normal protests of ecstasy: the first mean 'Stop at once,' the second 'For God's sake go on and finish me off.')

Games of this sort are an occasional optional extra to all sorts of sex-play and intercourse, since the tied partner can be kissed, masturbated, ridden, or simply teased to orgasm, but they go extra-well in both sexes with the unbearably sharp sensations produced by slow, skillful handwork. 'Restraint' gives the receiving partner something muscular to do while remaining quite helpless to influence the march of events, or the rhythm and speed of stimulation (what Theodor Reik called the 'suspense factor'), and enables the active partner to push the woman, at least, to unbearable lengths (she, when her turn comes, can drive him frantic by spinning things out).

Experienced and unscared lovers will spot at once the context where bondage games fit. They're a natural in the sort of love battle which some boisterous types favor, where she resists as if she meant it: at the end, either he gets a half-nelson on her, ties her, and carries on from there – or she is still holding out when the oven-timer rings and acquires the right to tie him. Or you can play it less rough and draw lots or take forfeits – in any case you should take turns. The other context, for non-kid's games players, is simply on impulse. One or other asks, or says 'my turn now,' or the active-minded party starts in and realizes their ambitions. He may wake up and find she has turned him over and is just finishing work on his wrists, by which time it's too late to protest (some women can get a lot further than that, with a heavy sleeper). Or he can ambush her when she comes back vulnerable from a shower.

To make this work as a game it obviously needs to be effective but not painful or dangerous. Technique is worth a few words because this is a highly popular sex fantasy, which isn't included in square books, and some skill and care are called for. On any bed with four posts you can stake a partner out, supported by one or more pillows. This is the traditional bordel method, probably because it needs no skill. Extension like this inhibits orgasm in some people – many feel more with the legs open, but the wrists and elbows firmly behind the back, or by being tied to a chair, or upright to a post. The critical areas where compression boosts sex feeling are the wrists, ankles, elbows (don't try to make them meet behind by brute force), soles of the feet, thumbs and big toes (artful women break off halfway to tie these last two with a leather bootlace – if you doubt this, try it). There are divergences of taste over what to use for tying. Leaving aside kinks like straitjackets or boy-scout garters, different couples use leather or rubber straps, ribbons, cloth strips, pajama cords, or thick, soft rope. Straps are easiest for women who aren't very strong, or can't tie reef knots. They need holes at half-inch intervals. Triangular bandages are all right for quick hand-and-foot tying, but don't look very sexy – and it is the neatness and wriggling of the parcel which excite the active party. Old stockings are a favorite resource but murder to untie quickly in an emergency. Chains, handcuffs and so on are quick, but don't give any compression and hurt to lie on. If they lock you can't rely on releasing them quickly. The weird aparatus sold by adult-toy-makers is for the birds unless you only want to pose photographs. If you like it, make your own. For most straight couples a hank of clothesline is fine. Cut it into five or six four-foot and a couple of six-foot lengths, and use a lot of hand-tight turns – don't tie tight enough to bruise.

Some energetic people like to be gagged as well. As one lady put it, 'It keeps the bubbles in the champagne.' Gagging and being gagged turns most men on – most

BONDAGE *opposite*
The gentle art of tying your partner to boost orgasm.

women profess to hate it in prospect, but the expression of erotic astonishment on the face of a well-gagged woman when she finds she can only mew is irresistible to most men's rape instincts. Apart from the symbolism and the 'feeling of helplessness' it enables the subject to yell and bite during orgasm, which helps a total cut loose, unless you have a rhinoceros hide and live in a soundproof room. It makes prompting impossible, so that your partner's initiatives are outside your control. Most men who are excited by this sort of game like to be silenced thoroughly. Untimid women often come to like it after a few tries if they're the biting kind or like the feeling of helplessness – others hate it and lose their orgasm if they try it. A few like to be blindfolded as well, or instead.

It's actually hard to gag anyone one hundred percent safely, except in movies, where a wisp of silk over the heroine's face enables the hero to walk past without hearing her. This is as well, as the prisoner must *never* be made incapable of signalling if anything is wrong. A long piece of cloth, with several turns well between the teeth, or a small rubber ball fixed in the middle of a one inch strap by a nut and bolt (the 'poire' of French bordel tradition) are quite fierce enough. Adhesive tape will silence someone but is torture to take off. Anything in the mouth must be firm, mustn't block breathing, and must be quick-release in case the subject signals danger – from choking, feeling sick, or any other source of discomfort. This signal (and this goes for *all* bondage games) must be agreed beforehand and never abused or ignored – penalty for illicit use, two further orgasms. A Morse-code grunt, 'shave and a haircut, two bits', is a safe choice. The Federal Safety Code must be observed and displayed in a prominent place on the premises. This is as follows:

1 Nothing may ever be tied round the front of anybody's neck, however loosely, and even if they ask for it.

2 Nothing loose or soft, which can get into the throat, or in general other than we've specified, may be put in anyone's mouth, or over their face, and all gags or knots must be quick-release.

3 Nobody helpless may ever be left alone, even briefly, especially face-down or on a soft surface like a bed. Don't leave a partner tied and go to sleep, especially if you have either of you been drinking. Don't keep anyone tied up for longer than half an hour.

4 Play bondage games only with people you know, not only socially but sexually, never with acquaintances, and avoid group scenes. This goes for couples as well as partners – some people are careless, and others are sadists.

Apart from this, cruelty of any sort, tying someone who is
really scared of the idea, tight cords, stuffing things in
people's mouths, idiot tricks like hanging people up by
any part of their anatomy, and the whole Sadie-Mae
routine, which to straight couples is simply painful and a
turn-off, belong to psychopathology not lovemaking.
Bondage as a pleasurable sex game is never painful or
dangerous. It can, of course, be played simply for the

CHINESE STYLE *opposite*
Wild geese flying on their backs.

symbolic aggression, but at least half the payoff in people (and there are many) who enjoy it is, for the person tied directly physical, in struggling against restraint and in skin and muscle feeling, plus the release of any surviving childhood blocks which comes from having pleasure 'administered' willy nilly. It also helps get over our cultural taboo on intense extragenital sensations, which belongs in the same package.

Ropemarks usually go in a few hours if you've been gentle. Rope burns and bruises come from clumsy untying – don't saw through the skin, but be quick, so that the man doesn't get stiff through being left tied after orgasm, and the woman comes down to earth lying comfortably in your arms. You can be agreeably, adequately and symbolically fierce, whichever your sex, without being spiteful or clumsy and wrecking things. The right mix here, as in all sex games, is tough plus tender. If you can't sense how tough your partner likes it, ask, then subtract twenty percent to allow for the difference between fact and fantasy. Given these rules, any couple who enjoy violent lovemaking and like the idea could do worse than learn to make each other helpless occasionally – gently, quickly and efficiently. This is neither kinky nor frightening – just human. For the pièce de resistance which goes with bondage, namely *Slow masturbation*, see that section.

boots

Notorious sex turn-on for many people – the longer the better. Complicated symbolism here involving aggression (jackboots and so on), phallicism and the female lower extremity. Used to be the badge of the prostitute – now general wear for straight people: have changed places with corsets, which used to be general wear and are now chiefly a sex kick. Odd how the market in the respectability of sexually symbolic clothing swings over the years. One could learn a lot about human imprinting by plotting the prevalence of such preferences.

Good for dressing-up games if you like them. Not very practical for serious sex unless you keep them for non-horizontal non-bed activities. If your man likes them, try appearing suddenly in long, tight, black, shiny ones.

buttered bun

Woman who has recently had relations with another man: unexpected turn-on for some males. This seems to be a carry-over from a fairly general ape behavior, where sharing a partner is a form of bonding between males. Psychoanalysts have long since suspected that the motive in much wife-swapping (and also the attraction of the gang night out and of the prostitute, who is a 'shared' woman) was 'homosexual' in character – it's probably more accurate to say that it is an instance of the way in which primate bisexuality is used to cut down overt inter-male aggression. If the woman is your own wife, there is also a component of what psychiatrists have called masochism and biologists call 'stepping-down in the dominance hierarchy.' End of lesson.

chains

The tied-up, tinkling look – fashionable now, and they look well on naked skin. Some women like both the coldness and the symbolism, and some men spend hours locking and unlocking them – you could try them on him too for size. Uncomfortable and only symbolically effective if you want actually to hold a partner still, but they look fierce, and some people find them exciting. Bright tinkling objects turn on magpies as well as people. See *Earlobes*.

chastity belt

A turn-on for some people, they were sold in earnest until recently to 'prevent masturbation.' Like clothes, the real fun is in eventually taking them off. Many commercial ones don't even prevent intercourse. The kind with built-in stimulation, vibrators and so on sound more fun but cost a bomb. The genuine article, as used in the thirteenth century, wasn't meant to lock up the woman, but was worn by her as a deterrent against rape – the woman usually had the key, and some women were buried in them to prevent posthumous violation. The only worthwhile chastity-belt game is to try, when she has a period, how many ways you can circumvent a really tight g-string and both get orgasm. Male versions are sold and appeal to some people, presumably as a spinning-out technique. Expensive toys unless you want to make one.

chinese style

In the classical treatises, remarkably like uninhibited European sex, the best thing being the delightful names given to postures: 'Wailing Monkey Clasping a Tree,' 'Wild Geese Flying on their Backs,' for two quite ordinary positions (seated face to face; woman on top facing away). Main elaboration consists in various complicated mixtures of deep and shallow strokes, often in magical numbers – 5 deep 8 shallow, etc. Intercourse naked, on a Chinese bed, in the open air, or on the floor. Woman treated far less as an equal in sex than in Indian erotology. Mystical schools tried to avoid ejaculation (see *Karezza*).

clothed intercourse

Really a heavy-petting technique: she keeps her panties or g-string on, he carries out all the movements of straight intercourse as far as the cloth will allow. Favorite ethnologic variant, chiefly for premarital intercourse – called badana in Turkey, metsha in Xhosa, etc. etc. Odd we have no special word. Not reliable as a contraceptive unless the ejaculation-position is fully interfemoral, i.e. with the glans well clear of the vulva, cloth or no cloth. Some people who used this before marriage like to go back to it either as a starter or during menstrual periods. Inclined to be 'dry' and make the man sore if it goes on too long – many women can get a fair orgasm from it.

corsets

A turn-on for some people – luckily now confined to sex games; they used to be an obligatory article of fashion. Make a woman still more woman-shaped. Firm pressure on the waist and abdomen excites many women. Some men are turned on by being laced into them too. Probably work through tightness and skin pressure, but a lot of symbolisms are involved.

dancing

All ballroom dancing in pairs looks towards intercourse. In this respect the Puritans were dead right. The development of no-contact dances has come about because one doesn't now need a social excuse to embrace a girl, but as an excitant it need not involve contact at all – in fact dances like flamenco or the twist are far more erotic than a clinch because you aren't too close to see one another. At its best this sort of dance is simply intercourse by remote control.

Most good lovers dance well together. They can do it publicly or in private, clothed or naked. Stripping one another while dancing is a sensation on its own. Don't hurry to full intercourse – dance until his erection is unbearable and she is almost coming brought there by rhythm and the sight and perfume of each other alone.

Even then you need not stop. Most couples can insert and continue dancing, either in each other's arms, or limbo-style, linked only by the penis, provided they are the right heights. Unfortunately this means that the woman needs to be at least as tall as the man, while as a rule she's shorter. Otherwise he has to bend his knees, which is tiring. If you can't dance inserted, and if she is small, pick her up into one of the Hindu standing positions, legs round waist, arms round neck, and continue like this. If she is too heavy, turn her and take her stooping from behind, still keeping the dance going.

This is a private game. Stripping at dances is getting commoner in some circles as a preliminary to group sex, but it usually is only a preliminary – after a few dances the floor empties and the couches fill up.

Seduction, or encouragement, while dancing is a natural. In the days of formal dancing one used to wish that the girl had her breasts on her back, where one could reach them, but that would have made it too easy. Gentle pressure, rhythm, sight and scent, and a knowledge of remote-control methods are all that are needed.

Most lovers are against Paul Joneses.

discipline

Codeword for beating each other as a sexual technique.

There is a venerable superstition, starting in English private-school scholars and backed by a vast literature from Meibom's *De Usu Flagrorum*, that beating is a sort of sexual Tabasco, the hottest erotic condiment, and no way-out party and no wide-scope porn is complete without it. Some of this is due to the fact that specialists in this field haven't suffered under the handicaps that affected, say, 69 or straight sex – beating is decent and can even be done in Church; sex isn't.

Beating is a kick which either works or doesn't. It doesn't work on either of us, so here we speak from inexperience. It's a violent skin stimulus, and Freud has been fully into the symbolism of punishment which goes with this – his conclusions go a long way to complicate Skinnerian arguments over what stimuli are 'aversive' and which act as rewards. Quite apart from fantasists and talkers who are far more excited by the idea in prospect and retrospect than the actual performance, some people are wildly turned on by it. For others, who have a real problem here, it may be necessary as a selfstarter. Skin stimulation and the occasional spank at the right moment fit well into most people's repertoire. Most find that anything more is disappointing in proportion to the scale of the performance (and possibly conducive to the thoroughly mischievous idea that women, in particular, enjoy being beaten up).

DANCING *above*
Stripping one another while dancing is a sensation on its own.

As we say, however, the idea of being beaten un-questionably turns some people on, and if it does you could try it. If you are lovers and one of you wants to be on the receiving end, the other need not be scared that they'll let out the beast in themselves by co-operating. If one of you wants to beat the other and he or she doesn't like it, or is turned off by the idea, that's harder – probably the loving answer is to settle for a lot of let's pretend and not much actual beating. This is a clear case where if you can't communicate fantasies, you shouldn't be lovers. Play it through a few times in words during straight intercourse (see *Birdsong at morning*). When you try it in practice, if it's the ritual which is the exciting part, make that big – don't be ashamed to ask for this, or give it: play matters. It can be a naughty-child or a mistress-and-slave routine or whatever – if your partner's fantasy doesn't turn you on naturally, play it as a game and enjoy his or her response. If it's the physical sensation, rhythm and style apparently matter far more than force, plus tantaliza-tion and the surprise element when the rhythm is suddenly broken.

Start gently at around one blow in one or two seconds, not more; gradually build up force until it is enough to make your subject want and not want you to stop. For two-way traffic the result, plus struggling, should both look and feel sexy, not cruel. The sauna twig level is nearly enough for most straight couples, but people who really go for beating like it hard enough to mark the skin. You can stick to the buttocks or cover the whole surface – back, belly, breasts, and even penis (careful!) and vulva (put her on her back with her feet attached to the bed-posts above her head, legs wide open; start on the buttocks, then give one light switch or two upon her thighs and vulva to finish her off.) Or tie the victim hands over head to the shower nozzle and work over them under running water. For a genuinely decadent European sensation you need real birch twigs. Canoe birch and gray birch, which are the nearest U.S. species, don't grow in the West, so if you live in California and want authenticity you may have to vacation with a chainsaw in the East or in Canada. You cut 2–3 foot straight branches with the twigs before the leaves come out, tie them into a bunch, and wet them before use. If you prefer all the trappings, one can buy ferocious-looking whips and paddles that make a great noise but do no mischief. People who want the physical stimulus usually prefer twigs. Don't use bamboo – it cuts like a knife. Don't play this game with strangers, ever. Lovers have enough feedback not to let the most violent play go sour. And never mix purely erotic beating with real anger or bad-temper – it could be dangerous. A game is a game is a game.

EXERCISES *opposite*
Any new trick you try needs a practice session in anticipation.

exercises

The Viennese Turnergesellschaft professors tried to make sex into a form of physical training. Good general tone certainly helps, but it's equally true that sexual exercise tones you up better than jogging. Adolescent masturbation, if it's guiltless and enjoyed, is one of the best specifically sexual exercises, and the man can use it at any age in learning to slow down his response to a level which gives the girl a chance. She, for her part, can learn to use her vaginal and pelvic muscles (see *Pompoir*) 'by throwing her mind into the part concerned,' says Richard Burton. This superlative knack can be learned, because girls in South India learn it. How exactly they learn has never been written down, unfortunately, and the first person to teach this properly to women who don't have the knack naturally will make a fortune. Whether the commercial device with a rubber cylinder and a pressure-gauge helps we simply don't know, since our female half has the trick naturally. The technique to try would involve having a bulb in the vagina and a light or pressure gauge to enable you to know when you were doing the right thing. Anyone can learn to waggle his ears in any direction in 30 minutes flat if he watches the ear on closed-circuit TV. This makes us think that the commercial gadget is well worth trying. If she 'throws her mind' with him in situ she should master it, and he can tell her when she is succeeding. Sucking a large, strong Pyrex test-tube into the vulva without hands is another recommended exercise. Once learned it is wholly involuntary and needs no effort.

What we do suggest is that for any new trick you arrange a practice session in anticipation. The time to learn new figures isn't on the ice-rink or dance floor. The most common reason that an elaboration you both wanted disappoints, whether it's a fancy posture or some dodge such as bondage which needs to be quickly and efficiently set up, is the attempt to use it in actual, excited lovemaking 'from cold' – so that you mess about, lose the thread, and wish you hadn't bothered with it or blame whichever suggested it. The usual outcome is never to try again.

Not that rehearsal need be coldblooded or taken out of actual lovemaking. Anticipation being good in itself, you first fantasize about it, sit down together, plan, and rehearse. Then fit the actual trial-for-size into the waiting periods between bouts – when you're both excited enough not to feel silly, but not ready to go completely: try it while waiting for the next erection. Remember even Menuhin has to practice the violin daily, though in love once learned is never forgotten. If it works first time you should get the erection – in that case go where it takes you. This means you can rehearse something new for each special occasion, mastering every movement but quite deliberately holding back and not playing it live until the appointed time. The waiting will help when that arrives.

To practice things you must try in full erection, make the effort, and try the new posture when you have one – either without movement, if you are set on waiting till later, or switching after a few strokes to something else. Of course, if it takes over, as it may, you might as well carry on, and turn practice into performance there and then. For most postures you can try wearing g-strings, so as to get the motions without actual contact, and some people find this exciting in itself.

feathers

Recommended by some for skin stimulation (breasts, body surface generally, rather than the actual genitals, and palms and soles.) Try stiff wiry ones (heron or egret) or an oldfashioned feather mop.

femoral intercourse

Another dodge, like *Clothed intercourse*, to preserve virginity, avoid pregnancy, etc., in cultures which cared about virginity and had no contraceptives. Comes for us

RENTINE *below*
atly boosts intensity of male
sation if you get the tension
t.

under the heading of substitutes. Used from before or behind, or in any other posture where she can press her thighs together. The penis goes between them, with the shaft between her labia, but the glans well clear of the vagina, and she presses hard. Gives the woman a special set of sensations – sometimes keener than on penetration, so worth trying. One need not be so rigid about technique as were our forefathers, who had to try to keep sperm out of the vulva at any cost. With care one can do this from behind with the glans actually on the clitoris, with striking results. Good menstrual variant, or for at least a few strokes before you go in as usual.

feuille de rose

Tongue stimulation of the anus and perineum in either sex. Not unesthetic if you wash carefully and happens naturally in a lot of tongue play, but don't do it if you don't like the idea – or be afraid to suggest it if you do.

florentine

Coitus à la *florentine*: intercourse with the woman holding the man's penile skin (and foreskin if he has one) forcibly back with finger and thumb at the root of the penis and keeping it stretched all the time, both in and out. Excellent way of speeding-up ejaculation, and greatly boosts intensity of male sensation if you get the tension right.

foursomes and moresomes

Subject of a whole cult today, of which we aren't members, so we speak from hearsay.

It's becoming socially more easy to arrange, and personal taste apart we see no earthly reason why pairs of friends shouldn't make love together: plenty now do. Whether they also swap partners is a matter of preference. They would need either to be very good friends or total strangers, and we suspect it might go less well in practice than in fantasy – there is high impotence rate in initial tries of this kind, since our inhibitions are often more alive than we realize. Some experienced couples enthuse about exchanges. Others regret them as disruptive or don't try them because they don't want to jeopardize the extraordinary mutuality which grows with real and total sex communication. This wouldn't affect the mere non-swap type of proximity. Since friends already swap hints on sex it seems natural to demonstrate, and one can learn a lot by watching, apart from the turn-on from other people's excitement.

The famous one-way mirror scene is for real non-playing voyeurs or for birdwatchers who don't want to put their subject off. In fact it takes very little intercourse to make most people oblivious of their surroundings, though some might come down with a bump afterwards. Most men could take the social setting; some women are excited by the idea, others turned violently off.

'Orgies,' by contrast, need a hell of a lot of martini-lubrication, which is a point in itself. One can't shed two

millenia of preachments with one's underclothes. They
tend to be ruined by liberal intellectuals who invariably
end up talking rather than doing – and fall to the ground
still talking. Hence we can well believe that the best
orgiasts are the prosperous upper middle class, minor jet
setters, and showbiz. It would be interesting to see how
they manage, but we have a biased suspicion that after a
few goes for the hell of it they'd be as dull, or as conscienti-
ously jolly, as the non-sex parties given by the same types:
also that we get better fun at home, unless they are *all*
experts, which we doubt. If there were a top-grade sex
society, it would still either not get over the lack of
instinctive feedback between strangers as against real
lovers, or end up as a closed circle.

Novelty itself does excite – the key-club, draw-lots
game is an occasional in most countries and a religious
ritual in India; we suggest this is usually, though not quite
always, a secular male enthusiasm. We can't see any
prohibitive objection between real friends, if the women,
in particular, are adult, well-adjusted and storkproof, and
the men not simply trying to prove something. It would be
a better bid to organize this only if the women want to
draw lots for a man.

Summing up, this isn't in our view a high-grade sex
game but connected chiefly with self-reassurance. (All
too often the active personnel are those who seem to be
unsuccessful in intimate relationships.) That is a worthy
aim, but not the point of high-grade sex. There is no
reason why sex should not be social if you wish – whether
it's also promiscuous is a matter of taste, both partners
having equal votes on this, since occasional no-holds-
barred orgies are an important anthropological resource
for man, there may be a case for them. Usually the woman
partner gets shanghaied. There could also be complications and anxieties, but there always can be complications,
even at bridge parties. And we don't deny that there are a
lot of fabulous party games for such occasions that one
could devise. Oddly enough, regular swingers seem to get
bored with these after a few tries and go back to at least a
temporary couple-relationship. Remember, too, some of
your best friends have V.D., and that the Pill makes it
easier to catch it. Some groups have been brought to a
standstill, not by V.D., but by an increase in minor non-
yenereal infections. Try switching to an acid-gel or phenyl-
mercuric acetate contraceptive, or using one of these as
well, and wash with soap between contacts.

Adjusted people who try bisexual activies in a two-
couple setting don't, Errors and Omissions Excepted, run
any risk of getting stuck like that, though the bisexual
element is an important turn-on in all swapping. We all
have a counter-sexual component. Expressed like this,

FOURSOMES AND MORESOMES
overleaf
Once friends already swap hints
in sex it seems natural to
demonstrate.

without any anxiety, it's if anything helpful. If you fee
intuitively that it's better left alone, leave it alone.

friction rub

The original meaning of shampoo, which is gentl
kneading massage all over. Much more pleasant if yo
shed all adult inhibitions and rub each other all over witl
one of the non-messy scented lotions one can buy nov
for the purpose – a perfumery gimmick that shows a lo
more insight than flavored douches and so on. Sit or
something that doesn't matter and rub each other
together or in turns – sunburn oil or soap lather work we
if you haven't got a special preparation. This always end:
in genital handwork, then intercourse, then bath together
Semen would be the ideal medium, but it is too little anc
too late – bottled lotion is a substitute for this particula
fantasy. She kneads his muscles, with fingers and a vibrato
as well if they like; he concentrates on her breasts
buttocks, loins and neck. With practice these sensation:
are well worth cultivating. The Los Angeles massage
parlors may get busted regularly, but they have nothing
one can't do at home – apart from the fact that they are
male-orientated, not mutual, and lay on a whole troupe
of girls for every man. Presumably a devoted woman could
call in friends to help – or a devoted man, to make things
equal. This could make a good two-couple game, short of
wife-swapping, provided the couples like each other.

g-string

Useful sexual accessory – for how to use it, see *Clothes*.
For actual use in intercourse, as opposed to dressing up,
it is best to make your own. We print a pattern. White or
black pure silk are the best materials. When on, it should
be absolutely tight and skin smooth, covering only the
vulva and pubis. Cotton will do – nylon has the wrong
texture. Other materials can be used as turn-ons, for looks,
but can't really be kissed through – if you want to use
these, wear them over the silk 'leaf.' Open-fronted panties
aren't the same thing.

gadgets
and gimmicks

The boom in sexual apparatus is quite extraordinary. The
great exponents of this sort of hardware previously were
the Japanese: in a sex manual one really needs a consumer
study of the market, which we have not so far undertaken.

Judging from travellers' tales, most ethnographic sex
aids are used by men at the instance of women; they must
be unusually keen to please in order to bore through the
glans and fit a 'spritsail yard,' like the Kayans, or insert
pebbles under the skin of the penis itself like the Sumatrans.
In softer cultures such devices are external – chiefly rings

G-STRING *opposite*
White or black pure silk are the
best materials. The size should be
about 8 by 3 inches – according
to the individual.

which fit round the coronal groove, made of feathers (palang unus – Malaya), goats' eyelids sewn back to back (Patagonia), or little hair brushes. These things are in museums, or one would wonder if somebody was putting an impertinent ethnographer on. The remarkable thing is that they should stay in place during intercourse. Nearly all are damnably uncomfortable to wear, and either pinch or get caught with hairs.

European equivalents are warty condoms, rings and the like, and dildoes – penis supplements or penis substitutes.

Sheaths are straightforward – they come in all manner of shapes and contours, the aim being to roughen both the penis and the vaginal barrel. Some have knobs or fingers to tickle the cervix. We are at a disadvantage here, in that these are supposed to help the female enjoy, but we've never yet met a woman who liked them. They are not safe contraceptives. Some people who are excited by the idea, if not by the sensation, buy a full set, including all the possible variations of shape. They come complete with a drying frame on which they can be stretched for cleaning, and should then be rolled and powdered with French chalk.

If these appeal to you, they are easily made to your own specification by adding knobs to an ordinary, washable-type or round-ended condom with Copydex or some other latex rubber cement – 'brushes' or larger knobs are cut from foam-rubber and cemented on, and the whole confection well washed with tapwater to remove any irritant chemicals before use. The kind with a thick corona ring strike us as downright painful. They also destroy the direct physical contact which, in communicative sex, matters a lot, but they allow one to experiment and to combine sex with handicrafts – such sexual Easter bonnets at least add novelty if you like the idea. We think they are more likely to precipitate frigidity than cure it, unless novelty is your turn-on. Buying sex gear together from a catalogue helps some people to fantasize and communicate.

Penis extensions, which fit over the real thing, likewise; penis size, it can't be repeated too often, has little to do with sexual feeling, though a big one may be emotionally stimulating in prospect. A large hard extension can do actual damage. The most these do is to boost male morale, though, like a chest wig, one wouldn't like to be found using one.

Rings are another matter. These are basically erection-maintainers; where they work, they can be a real help to better intercourse by stiffening a part-erection after a full orgasm – this is achieved by slightly blocking off the veins of the penis at its root, to keep the hydraulics working. At

GADGETS AND GIMMICKS
above and opposite
Rings are basically erection-maintainers: the finest specimen we've seen is Chinese and made of ivory.

the same time, being worn over the pubis, they can also provide an additional pressure-point for the clitoris. The finest specimen we've seen is Chinese and made of ivory. The two sky-dragons are sporting with a pearl (the semen) – in use, the pearl is a small knob to fit the clitoris, the scales of the dragons open and tickle the labia, and the whole thing is held in place by a long tape passed through the hole, back between the legs, crossing behind the scrotum, up between the buttocks and then round the waist. The Chinese and Japanese also bind thin leather round the whole penis, or its base, and the Japanese favor openwork tubes fitting over the whole thing – in each case, pressure at the base plus roughening of the shaft and pubic area constitute the point. Others are belt-like devices which hold back the foreskin by pulling on the penile root. There are now several up-to-date models in rubber or plastic, which fit round the base of the shaft and have a clitoris tickler to supplement the man's pubic bone. One of the best is hollow and air-filled, so that forward pressure expels air from the penile ring part into the clitoral knob – this is supposed to give a very unusual sensation. It didn't do a thing for either of us.

Quite a few of the clitoral knobs strike us as over-hard to be comfortable, and all rubber rings are apt to pinch one or other partner. We have yet to meet anyone, male or female, who got much out of them. None of these things are surefire erection devices, and most work at all only in the absence of any impotence anxieties. One new arrival, the Blakoe ring, goes round both penis and scrotum-root (it opens and clips shut). This is supposed to stimulate the testes by forming an electric couple, but it may just as well act like other penile rings by pressing on the blood return – it wouldn't be much use in intercourse, but some people swear by it to maintain agreeable erotic sensations, and hence boost morale, during the day. To stiffen erection, a ring needs to go round the roots of both

penis and scrotum – some lovers use a turn of cord. Don'
tie too tight or leave on too long.

Dildoes are artificial penises of varying sophistication
(some include warmth and ejaculatory capacity, others
built-in vibrators). These go back to the most ancient times
and presumably have takers – the modern ones have
excellent texture. Most women do not naturally masturbate by vaginal insertion, but since the ladies of the
Turkish harem 'were not suffered a radish or cucumber to
their diet except it be first sliced,' some, with sexual
experience, evidently do – and the sight of a woman
using one is clearly a turn-on for some males. They
can also provide a second penis for simultaneous use.
Single dildoes with a harness, or double-ended dildoes
are intended for woman-woman relations.

Merkins are vagina-substitutes – traditionally a warm-
water container with a rubber or plastic vagina. Attached
to an inflatable plastic doll or not, we doubt their utility –
there is no substitute for what they attempt to replace,
and, like the traditional hole in a watermelon, the only
excuse for using them in two-way sex is if the sight of a
merkin in use excites your partner. Vagina substitutes with
a pump 'to enlarge the penis,' apart from bolstering the
folklore about penile size, are capable of permanently
damaging the natural hydraulics and should be avoided.

Chinese bells (now usually Japanese – rin-no-tama) are
something else again. These are hollow ivory or plastic
spheres, one empty, one containing mercury, and the
third a large steel ball and a number of small metal tongues.
They can either be inserted (in reverse order) into the
vagina or put between the labia. Some are single, eggshaped devices. Movement, including walking, then
produces a quite unique pelvic sensation more inter-
mittent and intimate than a vibrator. Some can be used in
actual intercourse, others to maintain a steady stimulation
– all day, if you can take it. Follow the manufacturers'
instructions.

Skin gloves and skin thimbles have only just appeared on
the market, and good ones have yet to be made. These are
far better worth trying than any of the foregoing except
the last. They consist either of a whole glove, or better a
series of finger-cots the size of a thimble, each covered
with a bristly cloth ranging in texture from soft fur to hard
nylon pile with a tuft of bristles where the nail would be
on a finger. They are used for erotic massage of the skin
in either sex. With a properly chosen range of bristles and
some natural skill, these can produce an effect which
ranges from the pleasant to the excruciating. A well-made
set would make a fine personal present. See also *Vibrators,
Japanese style, Pattes d'araignée.*

Our final judgment is that unless intravaginal gadgets

help the sexually handicapped, which we doubt, they're a waste of good money. For most people, they only spoil the intensity of normal feeling. Skin stimulation is another matter. But we may be unusual.

gamahuche

French for extended pussy-kissing. See *Mouth music*.

goldfish

Two naked people tied and put on a mattress together to make love fish-fashion, i.e. no hands. Originally a nineteenth-century bordel joke. It can be done (if you are the victims, try on your sides from behind). Venerable party game, but don't play it with strangers, or leave the players unsupervised, even briefly. There was a nice spoof of this sex stunt in the movie *Soldier Blue*. A good many women can get an orgasm solo in this way simply by struggling, especially if you put them in front of a mirror. Don't both tie yourselves, even if you can manage it – you might not be able to get loose.

grope suit

Diabolically ingenious gadget which has just come on the Scandinavian market to induce continuous female orgasm – unlike most such devices it works, at least on any woman who doesn't shy off it as mechanical. Consists of a very tight rubber g-string with a thick phallic plug which fits in the vagina and a roughened knob over the clitoris. The bra has small toothed recesses in the cups which grip the nipples and is covered all over inside with soft rubber points. Once it is on, every movement touches a sensitive area – the result can be unbearable. Can be worn under day clothes, if you can stand it. When it works, the effects on the wearer rub off on the male spectator. An amusing, and expensive, stunt, but we think it would cut down normal sensitivity if used too often. Its main attraction is novelty – might make an anniversary present. There is no male equivalent.

Less blatant clothing which maintains continuous sexual excitement is an old human expedient, and well worth experimenting with. Most of it is designed for women, not out of male chauvinism but simply because of the difference in physiology: a continuous turn-on enhances the woman's eventual response but would tend to overload the man's and make him unable to perform. The traditional instances are geared to feel sexy for the wearer and look sexy to her partner. Some of them could be of real use in re-learning the proper sexual use of our skin. They range from long heavy earrings to tight straps, corsets and belts, rough textures (hair-shirts, bamboo-ring shirts), ankle-chains, footwear which affects the gait and

presses on the instep, and now, more explicitly, hot pan
which fit well into the vulva. See the full history of suc
devices in Bernard Rudofsky's *The Unfashionable Huma*
Body.

Most turn women on by their skin and muscle effec
and men by their symbolism, but some couples get
special kick by making her wear something wild unde
ordinary clothes on straight occasions, when one can't g
home early. Some commercial ones lock, and you leav
the key at home. Could be worth trying for men too,
only in the interest of fair shares. Continuous sexua
excitement you can't stop or do anything about would a
least make a dull occasion more interesting, and guarante
a good scene when you finally get home. See *Earring*
Clothes, Gadgets and gimmicks, Jokes and follies.

harness

Quick 'restraint' system for people who can't tie knots
bruise with rope, or like the look of 'apparatus.' Come in a
degrees of complication and for all postures – watch ou
for expensive confections which are really kinky-photc
props. Mainstay of way-out Danish sex boutiques. Include
some gadgets like the mono-glove which holds the elbow
back without cutting into the arms. Give very tigh
restraint and a lot of skin pressure which some people
favor. Some play up the horse-symbolism, or include
chastity belts, corsets, etc. The only really useful gadget
of this kind is the 'leg stretcher' – a bar of adjustable
length with strap collars at the ends to hold the feet apart
if you don't have a bed with posts.

horse

The horse is an erotic object (see *Clothes*) and playing at
horses, as well as riding them, notoriously turns some
people on. One aficionado was Aristotle, who is frequently
shown being ridden horseback style by a girl friend.
Medieval moralists who took this as an awful warning
miss the point. Men also like to dress women up as horses,
though they can't usually be ridden in this manner. This
seems at least as good a turn-on as disguising them as
rabbits. Mentioned here for completeness – it's not our
kick – but the game (equus eroticus, pony-girl game)
figures in the literature. Either sex can be the steed. Odd
how often children's games and grown-up sex games
converge. Some people purchase a whole outfit including
bit, saddle, etc. See firsthand description in *The Nightclerk*.

horseback

Intercourse like this is attributed to the Tartars, Gauchos
and other equestrian peoples. We haven't tried it, lacking
the horse and the privacy. He controls the horse, and she

sits astride facing him. If you were really set on this you could – in town – try a large rockinghorse, but whether it is worth the trouble we simple don't know. Quite a few women can get an orgasm when riding (especially bareback) and when jumping.

ice

The last material one would consider sexy – yet with its increased availability we keep hearing of people who use if for its shock-effect on the skin. One sex book suggests that just before orgasm the woman should slap a handful of crushed ice on her husband's back. Other people use an ice cube to go slowly over a partner's skin, including the soles of the feet, put them in each other's navels during sexual games and so on. Some women report

RSE   *above*
d how often children's games
grown-up sex games
verge.

using them for masturbation, even to the point of freezing an ice 'phallus' in a rubber sheath. Not so strange, when you come to think of it – cold is a strong skin stimulus. We see no objection to experiments if you like the idea – you will hardly catch cold on one ice cube. Don't use super cooled ice, let alone dry ice; these stick fast to moist surfaces and burn like a redhot iron. Test any ice-cube you use on your tongue, cautiously, otherwise you may be in for a shock.

indian style

Now widely familiar from the *Kama Sutra*, the *Kok Shastra* and so on. Intercourse on a bed or on cushions fully naked, but with the woman wearing all her ornaments. Many complicated positions, including some derived from yoga which aim to avoid ejaculation (see *Karezza*), standing positions, and woman-on-top positions (purushayita) which are regarded as specially devout, since in Tantric Hinduism she is Energy and he is Immanence. All, if you do it in the original spirit and not for variety only, intimately linked with the Indian love of living at several levels – not only sex, but meditative technique in which one attempts to be subjectively both male and female for mystical purposes, or modified dance in which beside making love one acts out a scene from the hagiography of Vishnu and his Avatars, or the Life of Rama. There is a section on sexual technique in the chief classical dance treatise – dancers were temple maidens or devadasis who gave themselves to the devout as part of a religious exercise. Difficult for us to recapture, in spite of a dawning awareness of the psychoanalytic rightness of much Hindu intuition. Specialities include love-cries (see *Birdsong at morning*), love-blows (struck with fingertips on one another's breast, back, buttocks and genitals), love-bites as tokens of possession, and erotic scratchmarks – much skin stimulation with specially-grown, long fingernails, from mere brushing to a passionate scratch (classically confined to the armpit and the 'girdle path' – pantie region – where marks won't show in Indian day dress). Of all Indian techniques the standing postures are probably the best worth learning, if the girl is light enough. Few women who weren't trained from birth could, for example, stand leaning backwards on feet and hands, limbo-style, then put their arms round their legs and their head between their thighs, so as to take alternate strokes in mouth and vagina – or manage the one-leg-standing, one-leg-around-waist poses cultivated by temple girls. The best Indian accomplishment, the full *pompoir*, comes from the Tamil South, and unfortunately isn't taught in the texts, though the devadasis learned it from their mothers. See *Pompoir, Exercises*.

INDIAN STYLE *opposite*
Specialities include love-cries, love-blows, love-bites as tokens of possession and erotic scratchmarks.

inversion

Not homosexuality, which isn't in our book, but taking him or her head-down. He can sit on a chair or stool and take her astride facing – then she lies back until her head rests on a cushion on the floor. Or she can lie down, raising her hips – he stands between her legs and enters her either from in front or from behind while she rests on her elbows or walks on her hands (the wheelbarrow). He can lie over the edge of the bed, face up, while she sits or stands astride. With orgasm the buildup of pressure in the veins of the face and neck can produce startling sensations. Unless you want a body on your hands, better not try this on a hypertensive executive – remember Attila the Hun's young concubine: but it should be safe enough for youngsters. It is the way to handle those idiotic women who try to persuade a lover to boost their orgasm by throttling them – if you meet one of these, never do anything so damned silly, but teach them this alternative and equally rewarding method. You may save two lives –

hers, and, since most people's grip tightens in orgasm, her next boyfriend's, which could easily be spent in jail for homicide.

Inverted 69 is described elsewhere (see *Mouth music*). This makes a good tryout, always works if you can lift her, and will give her an idea of the quality of sensation involved; not everyone likes it.

japanese style

Intercourse on the floor or on cushions, as with most Oriental styles: partial nakedness only, numerous squatting and semi-squatting positions, a lot of bondage, a lot of preoccupation with extras and odd devices. We're talking here about the sexual customs of eighteenth- and early nineteenth-century prints, rather than the modern westernised B-girl version, which is international. What would be hard to copy is the essentially Japanese mixture of violence and formality. Other things are: elaborate finger-stimulation of the woman, thumb in anus, fingers in vagina: and a big range of mechanical devices – a glans-cap of hard material (kabutogata), penile-shaft tubes (do-gata), some of them latticed (yoroi-gata), or with a glans cap as well (yaso-gata): dildoes (engi), often strapped to the woman's heel, while her ankle is held up to a sling round her neck to give a better swing to the movement: thongs to bind tightly round the penile shaft, rendering it both rough and permanently stiff enough for insertion (higozuiki), and merkins to hold in the hand (azuma-gata). Postures cover the whole range, but the lovers of the 'floating world' greatly enjoy the simulation of rape – what George Moore called 'furious fornications' – where the artistic emphasis is on huge parts, copious secretions and so on: sex is played hard in this tradition.

okes and follies

This, contrary to cultural traditions among squares, is pre-eminently the right place for them. The best of them, too, tend for this reason to be jokes at the expense of the square tradition. The finger-raising quality of lovers vis-à-vis society is as necessary psychologically as their tenderness to each other. That, and not just the spice of danger, is what makes love in odd places and under other people's unperceptive noses so attractive. This is childish, but if you haven't yet learned to be childish in your lovemaking you should go home and learn, because it's important.

One mustn't let the joke go wrong and sour things: if you can have intercourse in a public restaurant or on Auntie's dining table and bring it off, you can laugh about it after (but if you don't bring it off you'll be lucky if you speak to each other again). Most couples contain, for any

INVERSION *opposite*
the wheelbarrow.

JAPANESE STYLE *above*
aso-gata.

given occasion, one dangerlover and one restraining influence, and achieve accordingly a commonsense balance, helped by the angel who watches over such lunatic antics and protects lovers from the consequences. All in all, it would be stupid to recommend them but a pity to have missed them.

The amount of laughter you have in intercourse, pranks apart, is a measure, we think, of how well you are managing to love. It's evidence for, not against, the seriousness of your communication. If you have this, the laughs never fail, because sex is funny. If you haven't, you end with boxed ears or tears or no orgasm all round, through some remark 'destroying the atmosphere.' When it's really going, laughter is part of the atmosphere – even mockery isn't unaffectionate, and there's no joke like love well and mutually completed under unlikely circumstances. It's one of the few contemporary scenes which gets a laugh out of pure joy.

Taking a partner (usually female) around to square occasions nude, or in some kinky gear, under a long coat, is a danger-plus-snook-cocking game which some couples relish.   The danger is there all right – if you must do it, make sure she really enjoys it. The no-panties bit is dangerous enough for most girls unless it's very much their thing.

karezza

The Alice Stockham treatment – going on and on and on while avoiding male orgasm.

This is really an exercise directed against *Hairtrigger trouble* rather than a general coital technique. Long intercourse is great, but the aim will be to ejaculate eventually. Enormously satisfying for the woman: the original Stockham version, where the male didn't ejaculate but allowed his erection to subside inside the vagina has no conceivable advantage over going on equally long *with* orgasm, and is likely to spoil eventual response. Worth knowing about, however, if you read accounts of sex yoga drawn from Oriental sources. The old Tantric-Taoist system held that semen was spiritual gasoline – the man should be careful to conserve it while drawing 'virtue' from the woman. One ejaculation could dissipate this supposed virtue. Accordingly, a great many sexual yogic positions in which movement was difficult were designed specifically for this kind of maneuver – giving the woman several orgasms while the man conserved his semen and performed what was in fact a meditative sexual exercise. Adept yogis also trained themselves to ejaculate internally – an unrewarding technique which deposits the semen in the bladder, whence it is passed with the urine: occasionally the same trick appears spontaneously as a disability and is difficult to unlearn. This explains the low male satisfaction value of many of the most elaborate Hindu positions. If you intend to use intercourse as a meditative technique, you may well use them, but there seems no rational ground against eventual ejaculation in any case.

Karezza was developed, possibly with similar ideas, by the Oneida community: it also kept conceptions down, albeit not over-reliably, as semen can leak without ejaculation. There was recently an offbeat French priest who canvassed the same idea as an answer to Vatican scruples over birth control, under the title of *continence conjugale*, but he has been put down. The method consists in total control of male movement – allowing the woman internal movements only, and the man sufficient strokes to maintain erection, stopping as soon as tension mounts. Use it solely as a training technique for long intercourse, then switch to full movement and mutual orgasm, for which the woman will be fully ready. See *Pompoir*.

leather

Probably the most popular super-skin turn-on: black hide also looks aggressive or scarey and, being skin, all leather fixes natural sex odors. Unlike rubber you can now wear it fashionably without being thought kinky, which yet another example of the arbitrary social choice of sex turn-ons in clothing. Some men like women encased in it: those who like the ferocious buckled-up look don't go for wet-look, soft leather, and vice-versa. If your partner likes it on you, let him or her do the buying. This is one object turn-on which women respond to as well as men, especially if it feels and smells right – soft leather jock-straps seem to please some people of both sexes. Don't pay racketeer prices, however; most of the elaborate gear in fetishistic toy-shops can be improvized, though if you want an Avengers suit you'll have to pay to have it made. See *Boots, Clothes*. Even if the texture doesn't appeal, try a leather-based (*cuir de Russie*) perfume – it is probably the closest to the normal female attractant odor.

masks

These excite some people: if this seems odd, remember that they are the oldest human device for getting mystical as well as sexual inspiration, by making the wearer menacing, other than themselves, and 'possessed' by the mask, and by altering the body image through partial sensory deprivation. There are inflatable helmets on the market which accentuate this last effect. We find sex better without our head in a bag. Putting the girl's panties over the man's head, an old professional trick, works on quite a different basis (see *Clothes*). Masks, like corsets, were once a general fashion. Don't fool around with plastic bags – these are dangerous and obstruct breathing.

mirrors

These have always been an important part of sexual furniture in any bedroom not wholly devoted to sleeping. They turn love into a viewing occasion without loss of privacy and help the mise-au-point at a practical level. They also provide a turn-on by letting you see yourselves – he can see his own erection and movements without stopping. She may be turned-on by seeing her own body, watching herself masturbate, seeing herself bound, or any of the other fantasies one can enact, so that both get viewer as well as participant pleasure. Those who don't like them, by contrast, say they spoil the shut-in, non-spectator feeling they need to appreciate sensation to the full, and make the bedroom less like a womb with twins in it and more like Tiffany's. If you have never made love in front of a big mirror, try it. You really need more than one to enable both to see clearly without having to shift around. The exercise is worth it, not only for voyeur effect but to show you how unridiculous you look making love. Sex in cold blood description sounds undignified, but seen as one participates it is natural, attractive and formally beautiful to a morale-boosting extent, even if you aren't beautiful figures. If there does come a time when it's better to feel than look, we haven't reached it yet, in middle-age.

What you have on your premises is your business, but if you want to entertain guests, have the mirrors inside cupboard doors or on a stand. With all the publicity given to the one-way variety some couples are inhibited by anything they can't walk behind.

Old-style bordels went in for rooms of a hundred mirrors. Expense apart, these may or may not work for you; 100 couples acting in unison may be your turn-on, or they may remind you of Red Square on Mayday or an instant Roman orgy rather than lovemaking.

motorcars

These approach our ideal form of locomotion, the 'double bed with an outboard motor.' Big American cars come very close to it (there is room to lie flat, even on the rear seat) – Volkswagens call for neat handling of anything more than breast-and-petting work. The classical postures (she on the back seat, he kneeling between her legs, or both sitting, her legs round his waist) were developed for use by Emma Bovary in hansom cabs. All cars, whether adapted to petting or coition, have greenhouse-like properties unless you live in a climate where the windows quickly mist over. If you rely on condensation it is still a good idea to have a powerful light ready to dazzle cops or

MIRRORS *opposite*
Sex seen as one participates is natural, attractive and formally beautiful to a morale-boosting extent, even if you aren't beautiful figures.

prowlers – a really bright one will give you time to get dressed before sight returns.

For alfresco love the least-screened parking site is the safest, like a French eighteenth-century bower, because you can't be crept up on. If you want to do much of this, buy a small van, or one of those mini-campers known as adultery wagons, which are in effect mobile houses. It takes confidence to strip naked in any of these. For security the best ploy is to make it a foursome, taking it in turns while the other couple drive, or sit stonily in front behaving themselves and providing cover. Mutual masturbation while driving, and trying to score number of orgasms per gallon, are popular fantasies, but against the interest of safe driving. Seatbelts can be worn, or you can tie the non-driving party to his or her seat and work slowly.

motorcycle

Increasingly popular sexual venue, which combines the symbolism of the horse with leather gear, danger and acceleration. Has serious safety drawbacks, calls for the wearing of a hard hat, and you can't rely on the machine to look after itself as a horse can, but if you have access to a private road the hazards are yours. Better not attempted on the public highway. Another limitation comes from the fact that the woman usually sits behind, and you can't, or shouldn't, drive with one on your lap – clothed or not. Probably better as a preliminary to love than a venue for it. Don't let her liking for increased G override your judgment. Nobody looks virile with a broken neck.

open air

Countries with a warm summer have advantages which can't be overstated. In England, to have regular and full love out of doors you need to be frostproof and own a park. In Ireland or Spain, even though it is warm in Spain, you need to be priest-proof as well. Most parts of the U.S. should count their blessings. What is odd is that they don't do more about garden design. The walled or hedged gardens of Europe are nearly all practicable, at least by night.

Outdoor locations in wild areas are often flawed by vermin, ranging from ants and mosquitos to rattlesnakes and officious cops. Surface-wise the best venue is often sand dunes, which give shelter and keep the heat, besides not harboring stinging insects. Lawn grass is fine if well-screened. The safest cover, if you intend to strip right off, is the thicket standing on its own, where you can see out but they can't see in, the 'bower' of Fontainebleau painters. Europeans, who live in crowded landscapes, are adept at quick dressing and using places like Hampstead Heath and the Prater. With so much of America to choose from, there should be no problem – if you do take risks, however, cultivate the quick getaway and the weather-eye open; danger turns some people on, and others, of both sexes, right off. Enthusiastic larks one gets lost in, like stripping right off or tying each other to trees, call for very remote areas or a walled garden.

What you can do safely in Hyde Park, London, would be asking for gang-rape in Central Park, New York. When traveling, Catholic countries are more up-tight than Protestant, and Stalinist than other-style Marxist such as Jugoslavia, but anyhow you don't want to offend local feeling. A flat roof at night is a standard Oriental venue – you can make love and see the whole city.

Ultimately there will be scheduled areas – we give it another five or six years.

pattes d'araignée

Pattes d'araignée, literally spider's legs, is tickling erotic massage, using the pulps of the fingers, with the *lightest possible* touch, aiming to stimulate not so much the skin as the almost invisible skin-hairs: not on the genitals, but all the next most sensitive places – nipples and around, neck, chest, belly, insides of arms and thighs, armpits, hollow of the back, soles and palms, scrotum, space between it and the anus. Use both hands; keep a steady progression of movement going with one, and make surprise attacks with the other. The whole essence is in the extreme lightness of the touch – more electric than tickling. Feathers, bristlegloves or vibrators give a quite different sensation. If you are agile, don't forget you have toes as well as fingers and hair in various places, including eyelids, to vary the sensation. A set of finger-cots with textures from cardcloth to mink are easy to use; the real and original French style with fingertips is difficult to learn but unforgettable by either sex. It's one of the two general skin stimulants (the other is the *Tongue bath*) which work even on not very skin-conscious males.

pompoir

The most sought-after feminine sexual response of all. 'She must . . . close and constrict the Yoni until it holds the Lingam as with a finger, opening and shutting at her pleasure, and finally acting as the hand of the Gopala-girl who milks the cow. This can be learned only by long practice, and especially by throwing the will into the part affected, even as men endeavor to sharpen their hearing . . . Her husband will then value her above all women, nor would he exchange her for the most beautiful queen in the Three Worlds. . . Among some races the constrictor vaginae muscles are abnormally developed. In Abyssinia, for instance, a woman can so exert them as to cause pain

PEN AIR   *overleaf*
 you do take risks, cultivate the
uick getaway and the weather-
ye open.

to a man, and, when sitting on his thighs, she can induce orgasm without moving any other part of her person. Such an artist is called by the Arabs Kabbazah, literally, a holder, and it is not surprising that slave dealers pay large sums for her.' Thus Richard Burton. It has nothing to do with 'race' but a lot to do with practice. See *Exercises*.

pornography

Name given to any sexual literature somebody is trying to suppress. Most normal people enjoy looking at sex books and reading sex fantasies, which is why abnormal people have to spend so much time and money suppressing them. The only drawback of the commercial stuff is that because it is based on fantasy, and often inexperienced fantasy at that, it's not much help with sex practice. Depiction of any of the range of sex behaviors we've described helps people to visualize them; porno stories tend to be dull, repetitive, and a strain on credulity: frankly antisocial fantasies about torture and so on worry legislators and others for fear they might induce idiots to imitate them – it's equally possible that by enabling not very bright people to fantasize their unacceptable needs vividly they help to keep them from acting them out, but there is no good evidence one way or another.

Straight couples can use 'pornography' constructively in the exact proportion that it's well done, i.e. it describes feasible, acceptable and pleasurable sex activities they'd enjoy, or fantasies which, though not feasible, turn them on. This is what literature in general does. Many people, male and female, find sex books a real help in raising the level of feeling to bedpoint. Use them as football enthusiasts use books about football – even if the players in the story show superhuman shooting-powers. It isn't true that only men are turned on by sexual literature: it is true that women are most turned on by it if it's written with awareness of other than male feelings.

If you've got literary or artistic ability, use it to express your own fantasies to the full, for private use between you. Most of the squarest writers and artists have done this, even if they didn't publish the results. It's one way of dealing with the things you can't, or wouldn't wish, to do in fact – a kind of accessory to dreams and to play.

The idea of children getting hold of pornography terrifies some people. If it deals simply with normal lovemaking, this fear is probably not justified – young children are likely to be bored: the main objection lies in how badly most of the Mafia stuff is produced – some is enough to put adults off. Some adult fantasy-material, if it's odd or cruel, could be actively frightening, though no more so than non-sex material such as newsreels or religious books. If you do see your children with pornography, remember far more harm would be caused by any uproar you make about it. For adolescents it's probably innocuous unless they're obviously very disturbed over sex.

postillionage

Putting a finger in or on your partner's anus just before orgasm. Popular in French erotic books, and works on some people. Most prefer firm finger pressure just in front of the anus; in men this can produce an erection used alone. Use a small vibrator rather than a finger if you prefer – don't put it into the vagina afterwards, if you've actually inserted it. Firm pressure with a heel behind the scrotum or between anus and vulva works as well in some postures.

railways

An old and favored site for 'different' sex – now going out, as they won't let you fly united. This means, of course, the oldstyle wagon-lit or roomette. Whether it's the motion and acceleration or the association with love on the run that provides the turn-on isn't clear: it used to be fashionable in the classier Parisian and Viennese bordels to have a compartment fitted up, complete with train effects and noises, and vibrated by a motor and cams. Since it is probably the motion and variable G which score, choose a hard couch and a winding track with numerous intersections and switches. In emergency there is just room for an upright in the washroom.

remote control

It's an old story that you can seduce a complete novice, who has no idea what you mean, by slipping a thumb into a closed fist, or between your lips, and absent mindedly moving it in and out, in and out. We'd like to see this. All of the people we have seen it work on have known very well what it was all about.

This is one version of the pompido telecommando. The lip one works better, nail downwards in the appropriate rhythm – she will feel it where she should. She can do the same 'at' him, for example in eating (see that wild sequence in *Tom Jones*). Once habituated to either of these tele-control devices, most girls and some men can be radio-controlled as to excitement, erection and even orgasm – even by rubbing the lobe of one's ear – from several places down a table, the opposite side of a room, or the opposite box at a theater. The funniest use we've seen of this was when the lady was dancing with someone else, who spotted what was going on in his arms but thought he was the source of the signals – which actually came from her lover, who was sitting out.

The original telecommando is the 'blower' which

connects the restaurant with the kitchen downstairs. Appropriate.

rocking chair

Tried by some as an indoor substitute for that classic piece of sexual gear, the swing. Actually it feels quite different, lacking the sudden bellydropping acceleration which is the source of the swing's effects on women, but more like the sensation of love in a train (see *Railways*).

It works best with an ill-made chair on a very hard, rough floor – better, an erotic rocking chair with a dozen flats or studs on each rocker, hard cushions and no arms. This still needs a hard, preferably stone, floor and is infernally noisy – useless for an apartment if people live under. Normally you sit astride facing, but other positions are possible. We've seen a stool with a powerful vibrator in the top cushion which looks worth a trial, though the feel would be quite different.

rubber

This turns some people on, and is a wholetime fetish with others. Effect seems to depend on its status as super-skin combined with tightness and odor. The odor of latex rubber excites a lot of people if they have come to associate it with using condoms – it also enhances the normal female perfume. Wash anything rubber in soapy water, dry, and keep in french chalk – this includes condoms, ticklers, g-strings and larger items. Black seems to be the preferred sexual color. The livid pink condoms sold in some places don't look as good as the normal translucent variety.

Rubber clothes are one of the few very common turn-ons which for some reason, if you leave out skin-diving and water-skiing, have never got to be fashionable, probably because it's not specially empathic for women (or because it's unbelievably hot).

saxonus

Coitus saxonus – pressing firmly on the male urethra near the root of the penis to prevent ejaculation and (hopefully) conception. No use as a contraceptive, since sperms are around long before he ejaculates – but some women do have the knack, during masturbation, of stopping and restarting ejaculation by urethral pressure so as to spin out the male peak. This is best done by pressing on the shaft near the root with two or three fingers, but you need to press hard (don't bruise). Some people press midway between scrotum and anus. The idea is to allow ejaculation to occur piecemeal. If you stop it altogether, he will eventually ejaculate into the bladder. There's no evidence that this is harmful unless done

ROCKING CHAIR *opposite*
Like the sensation of love in a train.

violently and often, but it's probably better avoided. Interrupting ejaculation is also probably harmless but it is difficult, and won't work on everyone. Women who have this as a party piece say it is appreciated, but that may depend on their partner. You might as well stop just short of ejaculation, then restart the whole business a few minutes later.

shoes

A sex turn-on connected with the foot-pussy equivalence we've mentioned elsewhere (see *Feet*); symbols apart it's interesting that shoe-leather 'fixes' from sweat exactly the same fatty-acids which are present in the vagina and turn on male sex behavior in monkeys and apes. Though these smell rancid rather than sexy, they may still have a subliminal turn-on effect in man. High heels attract some males, chiefly for their effect in increasing the wobble in the female gait, another instance of making the woman more woman-shaped. Probably something of a hide-and-seek effect, too – Chinese women had to hide their feet but could show their genitals. Even for us bare feet are symbolic of nakedness, which is why lady pop-singers shed their shoes.

For most lovemaking you really need bare feet.

slow masturbation

Prostitutes aren't usually much good at advanced sex: this is about the one old-time bordel trick which is worth trying. To make it work, you need to know how to tie your partner (see *Bondage*) and to have a partner who likes struggling against resistance, but it works for a great many people. Traditionally, the woman does it to the man, but it works in either direction. You need good access and a completely helpless partner, though you can try it without if bondage games turn you off, but the result is quite different and you can't get so far. The knack lies in playing on your partner like an instrument, alternately pushing them forward and frustrating them (compare *Relaxation*).

The woman starts by tying the man to her satisfaction, either staked out, or wrists behind and ankles crossed, knees open, naked and on his back. She then 'signs her name' (*le coup de cassolette*). To do this she knees astride him, facing him, and performs a tasteful striptease as far as her panties. Next, holding his hair in her hand, she rubs his mouth firmly over her armpit and breasts, giving him her body perfume. Then she locks her legs carefully round his neck and presses her covered pussy on his mouth. Finally she strips off and gives him the direct genital kiss, (brushing first, then open, taking her time over it), pulls his foreskin well back if he has one, and stands back for a few moments to let him get excited. If she knows her job, he

SLOW MASTURBATION   *opposite*
The knack lies in playing on your partner like an instrument, alternately pushing them forward and frustrating them.

will be unable to move, while the kiss ensures that he won't lose the feel of her. Coming back she does the same all over again, stiffens him by hand and mouth if necessary, and starts in real earnest.

She has two focal points to attend to, his mouth and his penis, and the knack, during this warm-up period, consists in keeping both of them occupied continuously, without pauses and without triggering ejaculation. The possibilities are obvious – hand to each, hand to one, mouth or pussy to the other; varied by a touch of her breasts, her armpit, or even her hair. Between the two poles she will work over his most sensitive areas with her fingertips (*les pattes d'araignée*), her tongue, and her pussy – this last with one hand on his penis and her other palm over his mouth, never letting the rhythm slacken. If his erection begins to go down she stops, tightens him up

(this is the moment for thumb-tying if she is strong enoug
to turn him easily), then re-stiffens him. Then she ca
begin slow masturbation proper.

This is about the most mind-blowing (and, while i
lasts, frustrating) sexual sensation of which most males ar
capable. (If you still want to know why we include it unde
bondage games, try it for a few moments with an *un*
bound partner.) Sit well up on his chest, with your buttock
to his chin, and put each of your ankles inside the croo
of one of his knees. Hold the root of his penis with one hanc
and with the other pull the skin back as far as it will gc
with finger and thumb, thumb towards you. Then star
quick, sharp, nervous strokes—each one quick, that is
but timed at one per second, no faster. After abou
twenty of these, give about ten very quick strokes. Ther
resume the slow rhythm. And so on. If from the turmoi
under you and the general scene you think he is about tc
ejaculate, drop the speed (you can sense this with practice).
Keep it up as long as you think he can stand it. The
excitement is his, but is less one-sided than it sounds; the
male response is enough to turn most women on, and you
can press your open pussy hard on his breastbone, but
don't let your attention wander. Ten minutes is about as
much as most males can stand. If he goes limp, put him
out of his misery, either by quickly masturbating him to
climax, or by mouth, or by turning and riding him. When
he does come, get him untied as quickly as possible – delay
after orgasm will leave him as stiff as if he'd played a hard
ball-game.

The domestication of this experience, which veterans
will recognize as the Japanese-massage-special-treatment
routine, may be the one good thing America gets out of
the Vietnam war – the only bar to making it at home, like
sukiyaki, is if your are a big girl. The Japanese are artists at
making their knots, like their dishes, look really nice, and
Japanese masseuses are small enough to sit on a man's
chest without killing him. If you are a Brunnhilde, try tying
his legs apart and taking your weight on your knees, with
your pussy on his mouth: in the story Brunnhilde tied
up King Gunther on *his* wedding night, probably for a
similar routine – we've given the small woman version.
And let him try the same techniques on you.

The man has three points to concentrate on – mouth,
breasts and clitoris. A fairly tight couple of turns round the
breasts helps (careful!). He can start as she did, with the
coup de cassolette (armpit and glans) and then rub his hand
over *her* cassolette and put it over her mouth, to play
back her own perfume. He needs to watch from her sounds
and movements how heavy a touch on the clitoris she
can stand. He can copy the spinning-out technique and
excite her by postponement, but usually he will get better

results by simply pushing her as far and as fast as possible. If she is a responsive subject and not frightened of the whole business the reaction will fully test his skill in securing her. He should kneel astride, but not sit on her, nor hold her down – she should be quite helpless anyway. Finally, and with experienced lovers this will be when she is semi-conscious, he will switch to a few moments of tongue work for lubrication, then vigorous intercourse, and make her scale another, still higher range of peaks taking his own orgasm early on. He should know by the feel of her when to stop – this bears no relation to mewing and struggles, which reach a peak just short of climax. He should then untie her quickly, skillfully and painlessly, so that she comes back to earth lying quietly in his arms.

One unexpected trick is for the lady to tell her partner she's going to give him the time of his life, tie him, and then, when you've made sure he can't get loose or make a sound, make him watch while you masturbate to orgasm. This is more exciting for both of you than it sounds: he, if he's already excited and expecting something else, will go beserk, and his useless struggles will turn her on. Afterwards she can make it up to him – slowly.

outh slav style

Well-documented because of the very rich erotic folksong literature of what is now Jugoslavia. Intercourse naked, emphasis on the importance of genital perfume as a stimulus, several reputedly 'national' positions or approaches. Serbian intercourse (Srpski jeb) is mock rape – you throw her down, seize one ankle in each hand and raise them over her head, then enter her with your full weight (do this on something soft – the traditional bare earth is beyond a game). Croatian intercourse (hrvatski jeb) is a woman's ploy – an elaborate tongue bath, with the man free or staked out, followed after leisurely stimulation by riding him astride (reputed by local wise-acres to be 'exhausting'). The Lion position is a male masturbation method – squat down, heels to scrotum, place the penis between your ankles, rest on buttocks and hands, and move legs together. The style is passionate and affectionate as befits a race of bride-stealing warriors whose women were formerly, and still are, natural partisans: tough plus tender.

stockings

Can be a sex turn-on – often the preferred ones aren't the fashionable kind but old-style black stockings which look prossy. Tights are an obstacle unless crutchless, and only erotic, for most males, if worn without panties, and then chiefly visually. It is said that if you can get one stocking off her you're home. Actually in quick undressing or actual

STOCKINGS *above*
Often the preferred ones aren't
the fashionable kind but the
old-fashioned black stockings.

lovemaking modern nylons usually get ruined, but if you keep your nails and fingers smooth taking them off gently makes good foreplay, along with mutual undressing generally. Long gloves turn some people on – they suggest the old-style great lady. Unless you find shoes sexy, lovemaking is best with bare feet and toes.

substitutes

Handwork and oral love aren't substitutes for vaginal intercourse but techniques on their own. The listed 'substitutes' are what Europeans formerly used as contraceptive techniques which would ejaculate the male without masturbation and were less taboo than oral sex. The old 'substitutes' have their place – some, like mammary intercourse, can be fully bilateral and all are occasionally fun – during a period, for example, or if she is very pregnant. The *Paradis Charnels* of 1903 gives nine sites: hands (she joins her hands, thumbs crossed, fingers interlaced, and makes him a vagina, wetting her palms first with saliva – an old way of ending straight intercourse without risking pregnancy, though it isn't in fact a safe contraceptive method), mouth, between the thighs (see *Femoral intercourse*), the *Breasts*, the *Armpit*, and also the fold of the elbow and the knee. The other two substitute sites are the hair (long hair or plaits can be rolled into a vagina, or the penis lassooed with a loop of it, though some women may object because it's a bore to wash) and *Anal intercourse*.

swings

These are one erotic extra which emphatically do work. Swinging solo has given many little girls their first orgasm, because the acceleration produces pressure in the pelvis like nothing else. Swings are of two sorts – those mentioned by Eastern writers are simply suspended garden-seat beds, not capable of this kind of acceleration, but giving the agreeable feelings that go with a slightly unstable surface, the proverbial jelly-on-springs. For him, this is like having a woman with infinite buttocks, for her it is a swimmy sensation, devoid of the drawbacks of an over-soft mattress, since the actual surface can be firm.

The real high-velocity swing is the woman's turn-on unless she gets air sick first. The operative thing is the swoop, the falling-elevator sensation of negative G. Swinging with a well-implanted partner is a sensation every girl should have at least once in a lifetime: solo swinging with the Japanese rin-no-tama (see *Gadgets and gimmicks*) is another wild experience of inner movement. A plastic eggshaped saltshaker containing a really large ballbearing will do at a pinch. For intercourse, he sits on the seat, and she astride facing – he works the swing, or a third party pushes (traditionally the maidservant). Ideally one should try the Roller Coaster, but we haven't found a showground which permits that. On a garden swing, watch out for the occasional girl whose orgasm under these conditions is so intense that she blacks out, even if she doesn't do so normally, as she may fall if you don't hold her. Start at rest and penetrated, and use the movements of working up the swing to drive your coitus.

VIBRATORS *overleaf*
lovers often find them an extra
sensation to incorporate into the
ritual of skin stimulation.

turkish style

The Sultan of the Ottoman empire, so far from living 'm
Saus und Braus,' was the bottom man of a huge pyram
of functionaries and eunuchs, who lived in fear of his li
and was obliged to sign a stud-book at each act of se
Often he had spent his youth in the company of mistresse
known to be sterile, while waiting to know if he woul
reign or be strangled at the accession of another he
His innumerable harem were taught the arts of pleasin
but these are not recorded. The chosen lady would ente
his bedchamber naked, and in darkness dive under th
covers at the bed foot, wriggling her way up alongsid
him to wait his pleasure. Recalcitrant newcomers wer
brought in by the Aga Bashi with their thumbs tightly tie
behind, and frequently beaten into submission b
flogging the soles of their feet. Delinquent concubine
were drowned in sacks – silk ones if they were kadins. I
spite of the facts, Turkish erotic scenes were a grea
nineteenth-century fantasy in Christian Europe. They nee
not be so biased towards the male – she can equally we
be Gulbeyaz receiving a chosen Christian stud. Take it i
turns.

vibrators

A new standby, which have proved very useful in teachin
sexually inexperienced women to stimulate their ow
responses. There are two main kinds – penis-shapec
which can be used on skin, breasts, clitoris or deeply in th
vagina (the small size can be used anally) and larger moto
driven kinds as used by masseurs, which strap on the han
like a glove, and can impart wild sensations to almost an
part of the body. Vibrators are no substitute for a penis –
some women prefer them to a finger for masturbation, o
put one in the vagina while working manually on th
clitoris. Lovers often find them an extra sensation tc
incorporate into the ritual of skin stimulation. Vibratin
hotel beds, operated by a coin-in-slot timer, are also wel
spoken of, but are apt to run out at the critical moment
or make you ill. Careful vibratory massage of the whole
body surface is a better bet than over-concentration on
the penis or clitoris, but it requires skill. Penile gadgets of
various kinds for attachment to the standard vibrator base
don't seem to have much beyond novelty to commend
them.

viennese oyster

Lady who can cross her feet behind her head, lying on her
back, of course. When she has done so, you hold her
tightly round each instep with your full hand and squeeze,
lying on her full-length. Don't try to put an unsupple
partner into this position – it can't be achieved by brute
force. You can get a very similar sensation – unique

WET LOOK *opposite*
Try showering in a clinging cotton
shift: this both feels and looks sexy.

rocking pelvic movement – with less expertise if sh crosses her ankles on her tummy, knees to shoulders and you lie on her crossed ankles with your full weight. Why 'Viennese' we don't know. Tolerable for shor periods only but gives tremendous genital pressure fo both.

voyeurs

Title to be kept for those who treat sex as a nonplaying spectator sport. Any active player is likely to be fascinated to watch his game being played, provided the players are worth watching. Real couples are worth watching – the bored, semi-erected participants in blue movies seldom merit the trouble. Real human mating behavior is as interesting as that of birds and far more instructive. If you can watch others, do, unless it violates your sense of privacy. We lose a lot in this society by not being in the habit of making love in company. If we did, fewer books such as this one would need to be written.

wet look

Another super skin releaser which is getting popular – it makes you tight and shiny. Some people like the real thing with real water – try showering in a clinging cotton shift: this both feels and looks sexy. Transparent plastic raincoats worn over the bare skin do something for some wearers and spectators and are a fairly common male turn-on. Ask, try it, or both.

Problems
and what to do about them

age

The only thing age has to do with sex performace is that the longer you love, the more you learn. Young people (and some older ones) are firmly convinced that no-one over fifty makes love, and it would be pretty obscene if they did. Ours isn't the first generation to know otherwise but probably the first one which hasn't been brainwashed into being ashamed to admit it.

Some couples may be starting on some of our suggestions when they've been through the groundwork and reached the thirties. Since, however, we shall all get older, and superstitions still persist, it is worth giving the facts.

Neither men nor women lose either sexual needs or sexual function with age. In men, the only important changes over the first seven decades are that spontaneous erection occurs less often (accordingly they need more direct penile stimulation from the woman), ejaculation takes longer to happen, which is an advantage, coital frequency tends to fall, but given an attractive and receptive partner, decent general health and an absence of the belief that one ought to run out of steam, active sex lasts as long as life. In later life, the ability and need to ejaculate frequently get less. It's a good idea not to try for it every time, which will give you more mileage and no less mutual pleasure. Women lose their fertility at the menopause, but that in itself often helps rather than spoils their sex life. In fact, there is little if any physical decline in any attribute except frequency up to 75 and beyond. From a quarter to a half of all couples of this age still have regular sex, and that includes all of the people who never had much of a sex life when they were younger. Since continued activity keeps hormone levels up, for couples who make love often it's probably closer to 75 per cent and the other quarter will have stopped because of arthritis or the other ills of age, not impotence or frigidity. 'The things that stop you having sex with age are exactly the same as those that stop you riding a bicycle (bad health, thinking it looks silly, no bicycle).' The difference is that they happen later for sex than for bicycles. Over 50, the important thing is never to drop sex for any long period—keep yourself going solo if you don't for the time being have a partner: if you let it drop you may have trouble restarting (see *Health*).

Women can, of course, be kept menstruating indefinitely with hormones. There's probably little point, unless it boosts morale. A few find they get dry vaginally and need some estrogen, but in fact the results of continued sexual activity and of hormone pills are just about equal.

As with so many things, later life is the time when you've tried everything, and settle down to the things you like most – together.

bisexuality

All people are bisexual – that is to say, they are able to respond sexually to some extent towards people of either sex. Being 'homosexual' isn't a matter of having this kind of response, but usually of having some kind of turn-off towards the opposite sex which makes our same-sex response more evident or predominant. How far people act bisexualy will depend on a great many things, including the society they live in, their opportunities, and how far the same-sex part of their response worries them.

Being actively bisexual makes problems in our society, not least with the other-sex partner on whom, obviously, most of most peoples' most worthwhile sex life depends. We only include it in this book, which is about man-woman sex, because in threesomes and group experiences, which are getting more acceptable socially, 'bisexual' opportunities are inevitable, and a great many straight people worry – either because they find they can respond in this way, or because they are scared afterwards that they will become 'queer.' There is not much risk of this. People with a strong counter-sex bias usually recognize it early (and might be better not to cultivate it, if straight sex has satisfied them so far). Men, both for built-in and cultural reasons, probably bother more about this than women, who seem to relate more easily to same-sex stimulation in a group scene, and women exciting each other are a turn-on for males. Males in most cultures do, or would, play sex games together under some circumstances at ages or under circumstances when there isn't a cultural ban: apes certainly do. If we didn't have this capacity, humans might never have formed male societies, because erotic play between same-sex partners helps to override the rivalry and fighting we see in some other species. At the same time there is a whole biology of human sex identity which isn't fully understood, including the turn-on (releaser) effects of the partner having or not having a penis. Freud highlighted it, and primatologists are trying to fill it out. The point of this discourse is that same-sex play, especially in a two-sex setting, isn't 'unnatural' for man. As with other sorts of sex play, if it worries you or you don't like it, don't do it – but it isn't bad magic, poisonous or odd. Anyhow in a sexual mixup one loses count, unless one is vulnerable to such worries, about what belongs to whom. If you feel you are vulnerable over this, or over group games in general – don't try them. Straight man-woman sex is the real thing for most people – others need something different, but their scope is usually reduced, not widened, by such needs.

children

Children are a natural though not a necessary consequence of having sex. They impose responsibilities – not

least those of being willing to stay together and rear them, and of having to restrict one's immediate sexual spontaneity for several years. For most people, they are well worth these restrictions, but if you aren't prepared to accept the restrictions, don't have them.

Full blooded sex is not exclusive to the childless, but if you want it you must arrange your own privacy. Never involve children in adult sexual activities: militant and exhibitionist liberals who try to acclimatize children to the naturalness of sex by letting them in at any level on their own sex lives probably do at least as much harm as was ever done by the prohibitive sex-is-dirty generation. It is possible for your children to see that love and sex are good from their awareness that your relations outside the bedroom are unanxious (if they are anxiously demonstrative you will transmit the anxiety). What happens in other cultures is no guide here, because our society lacks their other supportive and educative mechanisms.

Most young children are biologically programmed to interpret the sight or sound of adult coition as evidence of a violent assault (they are aware of it earlier than you would expect, so don't keep babies in the bedroom), and the awareness of mother-father sexual relations is on all counts far too explosive a matter to be monkeyed with in the interest of Reichian experiments. Treating their own sexuality (masturbation, interest in the other sex and so on) with acceptance and naturalness is a different matter, but don't push encouragement to the point of incestuous interference with their private lives, either in toddlerhood or in adolescence, or you'll end up trying to use them to enact your own unrealized fantasies and turn them off altogether. Good sex education starts with being unbothered but not exhibitionistic, respecting your children's modesties, answering their questions, and letting them see that you regard this as a topic for pleasurable interest, naturalness – and privacy, not secrecy. Arrange the privacy with an eye to the fact that a normal toddler sees you as a rival, i.e. don't just lock him or her out.

Modern housing makes these counsels of perfection unless you are rich, but if you aren't prepared to make the necessary concessions, stick to having sex and don't have children. Nudity is another matter with which militant liberals can embarrass their children – there is a whole built-in biology of toddler response to adult parental genitals: we would say, 'Don't push it.' Children should see each other and non-parental adults naked, if the parents normally and unanxiously go about naked; but any element of a special educational parade is probably a bad idea. The good thing about family attendance at nudist clubs is that the nudity of people in general lacks the biological and psychological anxiety-overtones of

EXUALITY *opposite*
omen seem to relate more
ily to same-sex stimulation in a
up scene, and women exciting
h other are a turn-on for males.

nude parents, but don't push this either, and don't b
surprised or discouraging over modesties among you
offspring you don't as adults share. Don't forget tha
father's penis is a dominance signal and mother's vulva a
ambivalent object to the normal 3- to 7-year-old boy.
you are being deliberately emancipated you're probabl
overdoing it.

Preadolescent children should be told about norma
sexual phenomena such as menstruation or masturbatior
before they happen and before more anxious adviser:
(clergy, teachers and other children) get there first -
present them as what they are, part of the process anc
privilege of growing up: *all* sexual enlightenment, including
where babies come from and the nature of intercourse
are best given even before they can be understood, sc
that the child gows up knowing what is what, and proo
against scaremongers.

Egging adolescent children into sex experience is
pathological. By that age the test is whether they trust
you and are sure enough that you will talk sense to ask
your advice, but don't be shocked if they still keep their
own counsel. If you are anxious or see trouble, say so
frankly and directly, but don't bully. If you've done the job
properly and your kids are endowed with reasonably
good personalities they will have no less sense, if less
experience, than you have. A friend of ours found condoms
in his 13-year-old daughter's possession and phoned the
parents of her best friend 'to warn them.' Questioned by
her father, the best friend said, 'Yes, I know: I bought them
for her. She's going with a boy, she wasn't taking precautions, and I didn't want to see her in trouble!'

Parents whose sex life is really unanxious will probably
be good parents in this respect, but in our culture they are
rarish, and we can't help our anxieties. Not much point in
trying to hide these (many of them are built-in to man),
and play-acting, whether moralistic or with-it, is bad
education and is seen through by children. If you are seen
to be honest about your own feelings, that is as good as
you are likely to get.

Finally, anyone who deliberately sets out to use a
child or a pregnancy to prove something, to 'keep the
marriage together,' to boost their ego, or thinks it would be
great to bring up a child or children solo, needs to think
again. Of course children are ego-boosting and having
them is a natural part of being a person, but they are
people, not psychiatric procedures. Adoption agencies
are on the lookout for those who regard a child as a
medicine, a medal or a missile and screen them out. If we
could cut out equally motivated natural parenthood it
would make for less mental illness, as well as solving the
population problem in rich countries.

climacteric

Old name for the menopause, the time at which the woman ceases menstruation. Old John Fothergill the Quaker doctor wrote in the eighteenth century, 'There is a period in the life of Females to which, for the most part, they are taught to look forward with some degree of anxiety: the various and absurd opinions relative to the ceasing of the menstrual discharge, propagated through successive ages, have tended to embitter the hours of many a sensible woman – some practitioners, in other respects able and judicious, if they have not favored these erroneous and terrifying notions, seem not to have endeavored to correct them, with the diligence and humanity which such an object requires.' That about sums it up.

Menopausal changes are complex. The end of ovulation means the end of fertility, and for some women this subtly affects their self-esteem quite apart from any physical effects of a shift in hormone balance. For others it represents a sexual release, when they no longer need worry about contraception. While a few things, like irregular bleeding or hot flushes, are hormonal, personality changes like irritability and depression could be both hormonal and due to the fact that a milestone has been passed and one has stopped being young. Men, who don't have a menopause or any sudden hormone change, often, undergo a 'male climacteric' which coincides with realizing what they haven't done among the fantasies of youth, and that they had better do it now. This can lead to injudicious thrashing about, actual illness, or simply reassessment of their aims and opportunities very like a second adolescence.

Sex life for women doesn't end with the menopause unless they have been convinced that it should or feel they are 'no longer women.' Often it really begins then, if pregnancy has been a worry. Whether the symptoms are physical or mental, such as mood changes, hormones are often worth trying to ease over the readjustment (under medical supervision). The Pill can obscure the menopause by altering or suppressing the cycle: don't stop it until you are sure you are not still ovulating or you may get surprisingly pregnant. After the menopause, a few people need estrogen to combat dryness or soreness – but continued sexual activity seems to work nearly as well as medicine in preserving the function of both sexes far into later life. See *Age*.

defloration

Odd, how this major obsession of past ages has stopped being a problem at all. There was a time when it was a constant preoccupation for the promiscuously-minded male and a real worry to most girls. The change can't be

due to the shortage of virgins (there has to be a first tim
for everything) nor even to the invention of vaseline – i
more probably is due to petting (perhaps) and a change i
sexual folklore (certainly). Most girls are now carefull
stretched beforehand by considerate boyfriends, and th
others don't grow up on the stories of blood, sweat an
tears which their great-grandmothers used to tell. In th
eighteenth century a girl was disgraced is she didn't blee
like a pig on her wedding night; most modern lover
would reckon not to make her bleed at all unless she ask:
to be 'deflowered' in the good oldfashioned way. Even
then, unusual anatomy apart, it shouldn't hurt her 'more
than it hurts a vain young miss to get her ears pierced.

The first night is a special situation we needn't handle
here. Our point is that with the bogy of real defloration
exorcized we can revive the eighteenth century play-wise
and deflower her again as often as we and she like. The
Houris in heaven grow new hymens daily and are
perpetually virgin, but so is every woman if she likes to
pretend she is. It's not a bad way of celebrating an
anniversary. Real enthusiasts can do the whole thing
properly, honeymoon hotel and all; the result usually
works far, far better than a real first-shot honeymoon
One can even book the same room in advance. Or one
can do it oftener, at home, and at shorter notice. All she
need do is to say, 'Tonight, I'm a virgin.'

depilation

One way of getting rid of hair you don't want (see *Hair*).
Japanese women use a sharpened finger-ring, or you
can use chemical pastes (not round the genitals – they
often sting) or have hairs taken out individually by
electrolysis. This costs several dollars per hair, and is usually
only worth it if a girl has a lot of hair on her face.

doctors

There is no special reason why doctors should advise
us on sex techniques, but traditionally they often have
done so. In fact Avicenna wrote that it was a highly
reputable part of their job, because pleasure in sex is
'pertinent to generation.' We'd probably say that it's also
pertinent to being a whole person. In view of the clutch
of health worries about sexuality which we still inherit, the
doctor would be a very good counselor if he knew anything about it. In the past, particularly the Victorian past,
medicine collected superconformists with all their age's
anxieties and superstitions, plus a line of omniscient
homespun moralism which is still with us, occasionally,
over things like abortion and the Pill. This isn't the reason,
however, that so many people, not only with problems,
but simply with straight questions about sexual matters,

draw a blank from their physician and write either to magazines or to total strangers.

The trouble is that normal human sex behavior simply isn't taught and until lately, with researchers like Masters or Kinsey, it couldn't be taught because there was only folklore to teach. When we were medical students thirty years ago, not even birth control was on the syllabus, though at least we were urged to read Havelock Ellis. Also most of what was in the textbooks was tendentious bunk. The sort of folk commonsense which used to figure in ballads and stories had gone, and so had the worldly wisdom of eighteenth-century doctors like John Hunter. Accordingly with the best will in the world, a doctor who wanted to counsel on sex behavior either had to research it first himself, or read it out of one of the books, or go on his own experience – the last of these was fine if the experience was varied, but it could be limited, or eccentric, or absent.

We think this has changed, especially with the younger generation, along with the change in cultural attitudes, though some conscientious office doctors are a little inclined to realize their lack of background and push quite simple matters off onto the psychiatrist, who isn't necessarily any better qualified.

However, sex problems, especially if they involve health, anxiety, or you can't get answers from books, are well worth taking to your doctor. If you are making a choice, a young doctor who talks the language of today or an older man or woman with some personal experience (if you can gauge this) is the best bet. If you have a bad problem and get no joy, persist; if the doctor you consult is hostile or embarrassed, change doctors. Avoid evangelicals – Catholics have hangups over sin, but are often worldly-wise beyond their convictions. Shop around – medicine includes all sorts, and you don't have to put up with a Hippocratic oaf.

It's unfair to your doctor to take the Pill without telling him (if it disagrees with you, he'll have deal with it); to be shy of letting him know, for example, if you have potency problems (they could be due to medicine he ordered, or explain a lot of other symptoms you've been getting); or to be unnecessarily reticent about your sex life generally, any more than you are about your digestion. If you don't trust the man, he can't help you and you ought to change doctors.

excesses

Quantitatively, in sex, these don't exist – nature sees to that; the woman gets sore, the man can't go on. Medical and moral old-wives have spent centuries teaching that sexual overactivity is debilitating – they were never so admonitory over excessive work or excessive exercise and rarely over excessive eating, which is our mo dangerous hangup at the moment.

Sex is in fact the least tiring physical recreation for th amount of energy expended. If you are flat after it, suspec either your attitude towards it, or (more commonly secondary loss of sleep. Male lovers forget that wome who work or run a home or both aren't as fresh, eve though they are as willing, as the idle occupants of th oldstyle Ottoman seraglio. Girls forget that though sex i the perfect tension-relief for both sexes, preoccupatio rather than physical fatigue can cause impotence especially when it goes with a wholehearted wish t perform up to and beyond Olympic standards as a matte of personal pride. Different sleep-needs and sleep patterns, unrecognized and unaccommodated, can reall threaten a sexual partnership. Deal with all these thing by speaking out – being really in need of sleep only look like rejection or sulking to very insecure people who can' communicate with each other.

Sex commonly makes women langorous to the poin of sedation. It may make men the same, or boisterousl productive – in the second case get up, produce, and le her sleep after a suitable interval of shared quiet and love At night there is no sleeping pill as good as violent and shared orgasm – active lovers don't need barbiturates.

If ever you do run yourself into the ground, there's nc temporary exhaustion a few hours' or days' rest won' cure. Contrary to some belief, plenty of sex makes bette and better sex – it damps down overfast orgasm withou lowering the peaks: the terrific 'high' after a separatio doesn't depend on continence but on reunion. You car both masturbate daily while apart and still get it. Frequen sex also preserves function long into old age – not only i it a habit, but hormone levels depend on it; so, therefore do looks and vigor.

exhibitionism

Most people from babyhood get a kick (though not in front of adults) out of showing their genitals to the opposite sex – they are, after all, some of the best things we've got, and showing them to a partner is the start of better things. The self-adhesive label gets stuck on people who for a variety of reasons can get their sex in no other way, and show their genitalia to strangers. This would be a harmless but unrewarding activity (these timid characters are by definition not rapists) if people weren't shocked or frightened by it, though it's a disability to the fellow who can't get further than that. Under our extraordinary system, we reward them with public disgrace, imprison-ment, etc. No woman need be scared if she meets one.

There was a famous French lady who, when a man exposed himself, remarked 'Monsieur, won't you catch cold?' Exhibitionists don't commonly attack children, and wouldn't frighten them if they were sensibly raised, though adults making themselves look ridiculous, or behaving abnormally in any way, usually upsets them. Children are conservative and easily embarrassed. If your child meets an exhibitionist, tell them the unfortunate chap is stuck at the baby stage, and has so many problems they'd better stay out of his way.

fetish

Something you need instead of, or as well as, a partner in order to reach full sexual response. Less often evident in women than in men, so far as concrete objects or routines are concerned, though women can make fetishes of such things as security, fear and subtler nuances of setting. Can be of all kinds – embryo fetishes are present in almost everyone, and their satisfaction is part of the art as well as the function of love. Many men perform best with a woman who has a particular hair color or length, or big breasts, or looks boyish but are less frank about other turn-on requirements. Particular garments come next – she is more desirable with stockings, or with shoes, or with earrings. Use any of these turn-on circumstances to their fullest extent (see *Clothes*).

A real fetish is any non-sexual circumstance which is obligatory for potency. It becomes a problem if it swamps everything and develops into a consuming anxiety, (shoes only, not even women with shoes) or if it happens to be a fantasy which turns you on and your partner off, or if the performance gets more and more complicated and anxious until a halt has to be called. Normal marital play can meet nearly all demands of this kind if there is real communication, and find them fun, but the partner who is stuck with an anxious ritual can be a big problem which lets-pretend fails to solve.

For a start, a person with a real hangup of this sort, even if fully enacted, can lose interest in anything but his preoccupation. This is a medical problem, however, and time to shout for help. It goes with other personality difficulties of which the loss of interest in love is only a symptom, since most of us at some level have one or more preferred turn-ons, and, if we can't communicate with our partner, tend to get more and more guilty and sensitive about them. Discharged as play, this doesn't happen; but if they can't be discharged in this way, get help. We're talking, remember, about persistent and quite inordinate obsessions which get in the way of the ordinary business of intercourse—refusing to try anything but the missionary position is as much a fetish as only being

ITY   *opposite*
t suits a particular couple
nds on their needs, situation,
eties and so on.

potent when wearing a diving helmet. Normal sex involves both fantasy-preferences and variety – variety is the one thing the handicapped ritualist can't enjoy. There's not much wrong with anyone who is willing to try anything once.

It may sound brutal, but don't, repeat don't, take on a partner with a major sex problem such as homosexuality or compulsive ritualism in order to 'cure him by love.' You won't – though if he has your love and comprehension cure by an expert, or at least coming to live with himself, will be much easier. If you have taken on a problem of this kind – and the measure, we repeat, of whether it is a problem is whether it causes anxiety and interferes with sexual joy – work it out between you without fear or recrimination, and go to an expert. It's as much a medical problem as a slipped disc if it interferes with your mutual enjoyment as much as a slipped disc would.

fidelity

Fidelity, infidelity, jealousy and so on. We've deliberately not gone into the ethics of life-style. The facts are that few men and slightly more women in our culture go through life with sexual experience confined to one partner only. What suits a particular couple depends on their needs, situation, anxieties and so on. These needs are a particularly delicate problem in communication: if mutual comprehension is complete and ongoing you can count yourselves lucky. Active deception always hurts a relationship. Complete frankness which is aimed to avoid guilt or as an act of aggression against a partner can do the same. The real problem arises from the fact that sexual relations can be anything, for different people and on different occasions, from a game to a total fusion of identities; the heartaches arise when each partner sees it differently.

There is no sexual relationship which doesn't involve responsibility, because there are two or more people involved: anything which, as it were, militantly excludes a partner is hurtful, yet to be whole people we have at some point to avoid total fusion with each other – 'I am I and you are you, and neither of us is on earth to live up to the other's expectations.' People who communicate sexually have to find their own fidelities. All we can suggest is that you discuss them and at least know where each of you stands.

fighting

The occasional fights, often physical, which all lovers have would have nothing to do with sex if some couples weren't directly excited by them, often without knowing it. That real anger has erotic effects is a matter of true folklore. The

French have a song which goes:

> Hey, mister copper,
> Colin's beating up his mistress:
> Mister Copper, let them get on with it –
> It will end with kisses.

Or, as one woman put it, 'We found the old tendernes routine wasn't enough: he likes to use violence and i excites me to resist him. I find the pain exciting, but he' started to hurt me in other contexts and I'm afraid how fa it will go.' The trouble is that, as we've several time remarked, our image of love is up-tight about the very real elements of aggression in normal sexuality – whicl makes us prone to mix erotic violence with real spite o real anger, and confuse two quite distinct things, the quarrel which lets off steam, or is an appeal for help, and sexual stimulation. We aren't talking here about border line sadists. There are women who unconsciously wan violence (and have timid partners) who needle the mar into a fight without knowing why. The mixture is a bac one, and usually goes sour.

To need some degree of violence in sex, rather than the glutinous unphysical kind of love which the tradition propagates, is statistically pretty normal. But the way to meet this need isn't to use rows to fuel it, but rather to learn the purposive uses of play. True, the over-gentle spouse is likely to be blocked about aggression, and non-plussed by a demand 'Now try to rape me.' He's been taught not to treat girls like that – if he's excessively over-gentle, he may be sitting on a strong need to do so. But if these things can once be talked about, you can make him (or her) learn the uses of sexual play – which is why we've included some pretty rough-looking games by Marriage Guidance standards – and this without the need to mix them up with real day-to-day angers and frustra-tions which can get out of hand, especially with the wrong partner. If he's over-gentle, don't needle him, teach him.

In other words, don't be ashamed if you really fight (most people do) but don't treat it as a kick, or a way of turning on a partner's aggression. Use play, and keep it in the sexual situation. Remember too that people are different, and that aggression is now a far more disturbing thing to us than sex – so that a black eye is a sign of caring in one couple and ground for divorce to another. Cultivate pillow talk to unblock fantasies – ask each other just short of orgasm, 'What would you like to do to me, like me to do to you, now?' – 'now' meaning at the fantasy level. See *Birdsong at morning*.

Also, as nearly always with man, symbolisms are generally bigger kicks than over-literal enactments. But some couples get a lot of fun out of extended struggles, premeditated or impromptu ('love wrestling' in the old Viennese athletic tradition). Enthusiasts go in for elaborate handicaps: time limits, no-biting-or-scratching and so on. Most people find fairly robust but reasonable tussling quite enough, others play elaborate finding-fault-and-spanking games (don't play these over *real* faults). Women who dig an extra sensation of violence and/or helplessness differ whether they feel this more held down or tied up: men can take out quite a lot of the violence component in the actual process of penetration and working for orgasm. Once understood, none of this range of needs is scarey, and can be stopped spilling out of sex into cruelty, or the normal resentments felt by any two people who live together. Actually, it tends to discharge these.

Nothing we've said excludes the tenderness of sex. If you haven't learned that sexual violence can be tender and tenderness violent, you haven't begun to play as real lovers, unless you are people (and there are such) whose tenderness is abolutely unalloyed: these needn't worry about the risks of fighting. See *Bondage, Discipline*.

If you do have a real fight, make sure to end it in bed. At least it's the best way to finish.

frigidity

This does not mean failure to enjoy sex when one is dead with fatigue, when children are hammering on the door, in the middle of Union Square, or, generally, with the wrong man, at the wrong time, all of the time every time, or with the wrong vibrations. Males of the vending machine type (put a quarter in and an orgasm comes out) should take note of this. Nor does it mean failure to get a mind-blowing orgasm on every single occasion. If it does mean these things, every woman is frigid. Nor does it really apply to non-response if the man is clumsy, hurried and phallus-struck. We assume you know all this. Real frigidity is when a woman who loves her man and isn't consciously scared of any part of sex still fails to enjoy it when they've both taken trouble to see that she should. This condition, unlike male impotence, which can often be removed by simple reassurance (though not always), isn't easily helped by books. Female sexuality is much less arranged in a straight line than male – where a woman has difficulties of this sort they *have* to be dealt with on an individual basis.

A few cases of non-enjoying are simple; the Pill can produce big swings in libido either way. So can the woman's own internal chemistry, which is cyclical, unlike the man's, and undergoes more sudden changes. If intercourse hurts, that is simple too – see a gynecologist and have it attended to. Pregnancy and having a baby can affect response, physically and psychologically. Assuming

it's none of these, and you have a husband whom you can talk to and fantasize with, and you've eliminated obvious turn-offs like having an overweight lover on top of you, but still nothing really leaves you feeling satisfied, get personal advice. The mix of physical and psychological causes which can produce this kind of dissatisfaction is too complicated to be dealt with in a book.

The only technique worth trying, if you still don't feel, is painstaking self-education through relaxed, gradual and private self-exploration. Masturbation in women is far more a process of continuing self-exploration than it is in man, and many women can and do teach themselves to respond in this way. On widespread testimony the use of a vibrator helps – it can produce some sexual feeling in almost any woman. Once you have found a stimulus which makes you feel at all, whether you discover it solo or with your lover, incorporate it into lovemaking and use it to the full. If you need a finger on the clitoris, or genital kissing, use them fully – the propaganda about 'vaginal orgasm' *is* propaganda, and there is no truth in the value-judgment that unless you are fully satisfied only by deep penetration you aren't a woman; some women are satisfied by it, others aren't. Some women get many orgasms – some so many that they merge and can't be pinpointed as a single event – others get one, like a man. Some women only enjoy breast stimulation, or genital stimulation. Find your pattern. If you haven't experimented with changes of posture, do – by this time we assume you have. And with play and fantasy. If none of these things give you any lead you can develop, you need individual help (or more correctly help as a couple – if you see a counselor, both should go).

For self-training, start by getting really comfortable – naked or not, in front of a mirror or not, just as you prefer. Think and fantasize about anything which stirs any sort of response, then begin gradually to explore your own body, letting your hand go where your body wants it – breasts, the whole skin surface, labia, clitoris. Do the same if you use a vibrator – don't go for orgasm, but set out to discover what you like and what you think you would like. It takes time to learn this if you don't already know. Sometimes, if this doesn't frighten you or turn you off, another woman can help more than a man. That doesn't make you a lesbian. Don't assume that another man will be able to do better than your lover–he may, but it isn't a safe assumption. If you can imagine a situation which would excite you, try to set it up with your lover – as play, if it isn't feasible in earnest – remembering that fantasy-rape isn't real rape or fantasy-cruelty real cruelty. See if any of our suggestions turn you on in prospect. Talk to your man.

RIGIDITY *opposite*
Doesn't apply to non-response if the man is clumsy, hurried or phallus-struck.

Beyond that, we can't help through the printed page. Female libido is controlled, oddly enough, by the male hormone. See *Impotence*.

hairtrigger trouble

Alias premature ejaculation. Any ejaculation which happens before you both want it to is premature.

Premature coming results from two causes, over-eagerness and anxiety. Over-eagerness may be delightful on occasion, but usually means simply that you are not having enough sex to reach optimal performance. One can ward off this solo by masturbating frequently and using the occasion to develop slow responses, but in the presence of all the stimuli from a real woman this can still break down. Once you get anxious it can become a physiological habit like stammering or impotence. It can rule out top quality sex and most of our suggestions.

There is a set drill for handling this hangup which rarely fails. Tackle it early.

1 Find out, with your partner, just how soon after one ejaculation you can get another erection, either by self-stimulation or with her stimulating you. Use this, holding back deliberately, and aiming not to get an orgasm but to see how long you can stay rigid. Do this often.

2 If the time interval is too long or you lose the second erection quickly, you need specific exercises. Set aside a time for practice and resolve that on the practice occasions you won't have intercourse. Get your partner to stiffen you, if necessary, and begin slow masturbation seated astride. Her aim will be simply to keep you in erection, even if she has to drop her stroke-rate to one in three seconds. If you call 'stop' she must stop. She can tie you if this really gives her better control, but as this itself is an excitant it is better if you deliberately hold still. Don't be worried if on the first occasion you ejaculate at once – try again half an hour later. Do this just as often as you can arrange it, but intersperse with intercourse, however short, so as not to build up an appetite. Either in intercourse or for practice sessions, some people find a local anesthetic jelly a help, and if you find it difficult to get the exercises going, you could try this. In about three weeks of regular practice you should be able to hold at least a second, and probably a first erection, for a full five minutes, and this will get longer and longer. Meanwhile, try and lengthen the straight coitus sessions. Use all the extras to give your partner full orgasm as often as she needs it, but she should be sparing with very stimulating techniques, or indeed any techniques, ahead of penetration. Try holding still inside her for timed minute intervals.

3 If this doesn't work, or you are getting anxious, see an expert. Usually it does work. The important thing is to set up by agreement a definite noncoital session, designed to get you into a state of sexual training. You will both benefit, and she needn't go without meanwhile: learn to use your hands and your tongue and don't forget her breasts. Having times when you specifically set out to satisfy *her* will help you to relax over any virility problems. If the problem remains, take advice before it gets to be a habit. Most men with limited sex experience are overquick to start with, and would benefit from training of the kind we've described.

At the first session with a much-desired partner, at least 50 percent of men either ejaculate too quickly or fail to get an erection. Ensure a whole night, so you can try for a comeback, but don't try too hard. If you go to sleep you will probably wake with a huge erection.

Note for your doctor: Tricyclic antidepressants such as Tryptizol (Rx) or Tofranil (imipramine, Rx) slow down orgasm enormously in some males without blocking erection: minute doses are often enough.

hazards

Contrary to superstition, very few sexual techniques are actually dangerous. Clumsy penetration with the woman on top can injure him or her; violent anal penetration can injure her, and all anal intercourse carries a small risk of urethritis in the man, and vaginitis in the woman if you mix anal with vaginal penetration. Women liable to miscarry need to be gently handled in pregnancy, and women who are very liable to miscarry might do better to avoid orgasm while carrying. Apart from these there are a few tricks which are risky in themselves. None of these are popular, but clearly, since mischief is reported, people occasionally try them.

1 Never throttle anyone, even in play, and especially in orgasm. Many sex 'murders' are accidents overtaking women who treat partial strangulation as a kick: they can get exactly the same sensation safely by intercourse head-down, see *Inversion*. Never block a partner's airway, and be extra careful with bondage games – one can suffocate on a soft surface.

2 Never blow into the vagina. This trick can cause air embolism and has caused sudden death.

3 In spite of writers who talk about the use of household appliances for sex kicks, never fool about sexually with vacuum cleaners or with air-lines. A garage tyre inflator line has ruptured the intestine when squirted 18 inches from someone's anus (this was a practical joke). Vacuum cleaner injuries of the penis are surprisingly common and

very hard to repair satisfactorily. Water at tap-pressure is safe, but direct it at the clitoris, not forcibly into the vagina – anything under pressure can go up the Fallopian tubes and do harm.

4 Cantharides (spanish fly) is not an aphrodisiac but an irritant poison about as powerful as mustard gas. The dose which produces useless, painful erection by inflaming the penis is bigger than the fatal dose for kidney damage. Candy containing it has killed several girls.

5 Nothing you inhale is a safe kick: organic chemicals which produce dizziness also produce death rather easily. Amyl nitrite (used for anginal attacks) produces flushing and other sexy sensations, but is grossly unsafe to fool with. If you want to blow your mind, try loud music through earphones.

Considering the range of human sexual experimentation it is a reflection on conventional fears that only manifestly idiotic sexual experiments are dangerous. Given reasonable gentleness, sex play is by far the safest energetic sport – one can be killed dead by a golf ball.

health

If you're acutely ill you probably won't feel like sex. There are very few longer-lasting medical conditions where a prescription of 'no sex' is justified for more than a shortish time, like getting over a heart attack or a hernia operation, or, of course, if you have an infectious disease such as V.D. or trichomoniasis, or are pregnant and likely to miscarry. Most doctors know this, but a few still give alarmist or thoughtless 'no sex' instructions if their own sex-lives are unimportant.

If the doctor advises the woman to avoid sex, she should find out why. He may only mean that pregnancy would be dangerous. The same applies if there's a heavy genetic risk. In that case a thoughtful male partner would have a *Vasectomy*, to be 100 percent sure. Otherwise the only indications are the ones we've given. If it's the man who gets the red light, discuss it. Even severe heart or kidney illness isn't normally a bar to having gentle sex, nor is hypertension. In these cases it might be sensible to avoid very tense or violent activities. Excitement is greatest, and casualties highest, in extramarital rather than married contexts, and boudoirs and brothels have seen more fatal accidents than the marriage bed. There can be a problem over cancer of the prostate or high blood pressure, because some of the drugs used to treat these can affect potency, and if other types of drug fail to work you may have to make a choice. The important thing is not to take no for an answer unless you've had a full explanation and are sure the doctor knows how much sex means to you (some doctors still think that sex over fifty is expendable or non-existent – see *Age*). A good doctor will know that stopping sex for any length of time is hard for normal people, and can damage an older man's sexual response when he tries to restart. Really good and informed medical advice, by contrast, may be precisely what could help you to keep going and avoid further illness – you and the doctor should work out the solution together. Some people would feel that if the worst came to the worst, it's the best way to go, and the anxiety and depression engendered by a ban on sex could be more likely to do harm than the very moderate exercise involved in intercourse. See *Doctors*. There is evidence that an improved sex-life can actually lower hypertension where this is due to general anxiety.

impotence

The basis of so much nonsense and anxiety that a few facts are in order.

1 All men are impotent sometimes – usually at a first or a hurried session with someone highly desirable whom they want to impress. The risk is proportional to the buildup. Can also happen domestically, quite without expectation or warning – often from some turn-off one isn't aware of. The only importance of these occasions is not to be thrown by them. The conventional male fantasy of being ready to perform anytime, anywhere is wholly neurotic and impractical.

Only the totally insensitive are all-time fucking machines like a stud-bull, and stud-bulls too have their off-days. Leave yourself a whole night for a first night – you should wake horny.

2 Physical factors which cause impotence do exist – the chief are diabetes, obesity, alcohol, and some drugs prescribed for depression and for high blood pressure.

3 The only other common cause of impotence is psychological – turning oneself off by apprehension about sexual performance. This is the exact analogy to the old man who took thought whether he slept with his beard in or out of the bed and went crazy trying to remember, or the pianist who starts thinking about his fingers.

4 If you can ever get an erection (by masturbation, in sleep, or on waking) there is nothing physical the matter with the hydraulics.

5 Age has absolutely nothing to do with impotence unless it brings illness. Belief that one is aging and must run out of steam has. Normal male potency lasts as long as life. The only change is that spontaneous erection gets rarer, direct skin stimulation is needed, and orgasm takes

longer to come. Impotence in old men is due to turn-offs, lack of health and an attractive partner, attempts to perform too often, or the demands of a younger partner who sets them a proficiency test. These would turn normal people off at any age.

6 Accordingly, persistent impotence means either that you are trying to perform against a specific turn-off – wrong scene, wrong partner, wrong vibrations, record attempts – or that you are turning yourself off by acting as if you were a spectator, not a participant and worrying about how you are doing. This can start if you are badly put out over one of the off-days mentioned in (1) above, and can become a habit. Deal with it exactly as for *Hairtrigger trouble*, except that in this case both of you should use every accessory excitation but with a firm resolve not to have intercourse – full description of the technique in Masters and Johnson which is easily adaptable to do-it-yourself. If this fails, get help from an expert. If everyone knew the facts listed here the task of sex-therapists would at least be lightened by comprehension.

In a few people liable to erection failure male hormone levels are low, but this could be effect, not cause. Taking male hormone turns off your own supply and it can make things worse (though eunuchs stay potent, so huge testicles aren't essential provided you reach puberty safely). Some synthetic hormones avoid the turn-off effect. Testosterone does help significantly in cases of large unexplained swings in libido, particularly after fifty, but needs medical control to avoid trouble: male gonado-tropin also helps some cases, but would probably only be available from a research group. There are newer erection turn-on drugs which may eventually have a use; their chief utility would be as morale-boosters – once reassured that you can erect at will, the problem goes.

The Japanese have marketed an electro-erector which it is claimed will work on a near-corpse: we haven't seen this. On no account fool around with home-built electronics or the line supply.

As a final resort, it probably isn't 100 percent true that you can't will an erection. Almost all involuntary body processes can be made controllable by a technique called operant conditioning – one can learn, for example, to slow the heart or alter the brain waves. It ought to be possible to do this with erection, shortcircuiting any psychological hangups – yogis can will instant erection without arousal, so it can be done. But you'd need research-grade help until the technique has been worked out.

Note for the non-sexologist doctor: if you want a short, recent summary of what can and can't be done with hormones in impotence and frigidity, read R. B. Greenblatt, *Medical Opinion*, September 1971, 7, 22–26. Reading time 5 minutes. Mesterolone is probably the safest and most effective hormone to use.

infertility

A boon if you want it, a curse if you don't. Can be due to the woman not ovulating, the ova not reaching the uterus through tubal blockage, various conditions in the female organs; the man not having any sperms, or enough sperms; and probably also various chemical incompatibilities between partners. These can sometimes be helped by advice including concentration on fertile periods, surgery, or hormones, but need proper medical counseling (both of you must go – if the man has too few sperms there is no point in subjecting the woman to a lot of investigation). Anxiety can sometimes apparently block fertility – overfrequent ejaculation lowers the sperm count, so don't be over-eager. Tight warm clothing around the scrotum can kill off the sperms, which need to develop below body-temperature. Orgasm in the woman doesn't make conception more likely. Infertility can sometimes end suddenly after years, and the treatment or the life situation get the credit. Obstinate lack of sperms in the male is difficult to treat, though you can concentrate the sperms he has and inseminate with them. It has nothing whatever to do with virility judged by sexual performance. Never assume you are infertile unless it has been proved, and be careful stopping the pill around menopause time. For voluntary infertility see *Children, Birth control, Vasectomy*.

obesity

Fatness in our culture is unlovely. We know someone whose pretty, fat daughter can only get Middle Eastern boyfriends because of this norm. Renoir's women, who, when naked, look ideal for sex, would look a little too plump if clothed.

What isn't realized is that in men overweight is a physical cause of impotence. If neither this nor the esthetics of it bother you, you may still have to circumvent it. King Edward VII of Britain ('Tum-Tum'), had a special couch resembling a gynecological table made to enable him to get on target. Most stout men can manage with the woman astride, backing or facing. If this doesn't work, try lying face-up over the edge of the bed, feet on the floor, while she stands astride. An over-heavy man is a bad problem – Cleopatra could say, 'O happy horse, to bear the weight of Anthony,' but he didn't weigh 200 pounds. If you are grossly overweight, set about losing it, whether you value your sex life or only your life. That applies to both sexes. Modern girls, though supple, tend to be underweight by the sexual standards of the past, especially for rear-entry positions and for making love on a firm surface.

pain

Pain per se isn't a sexual excitant in spite of folklore. What actually happens is that once excitement starts to build pain-awareness is reduced steadily, until any strongish stimulus, even one which normally would be over-strong adds to the buildup. This can be true elsewhere – you can lose a tooth in a football game and not notice it until after – but with sex excitement the pain-stimulus can actually be transformed into increased pleasure-feeling provided it isn't too strong. There is a sharp point, however, at which over-stimulation becomes a turn-off, not a turn-on, and if this is overstepped the buildup collapses: tolerance increases the closer you get to orgasm – just before it people can take, for example, quite hard slaps – but the transformation stops as soon as orgasm occurs, so don't continue awkward postures or hard stimuli after this. Some people don't transform at all. If anything you do is perceived as straight untransformed pain it's either too much or too early on, or you've gone on after orgasm. Learning what stimuli are pleasant as buildup and what aren't is an art.

If any part of normal sex actually hurts, due to soreness, internal organs getting knocked, etc., you're being clumsy or something is wrong – in the second case see a doctor if it lasts more than a few days. First coitus can be slightly painful for both parties – if they are excited enough beforehand the transformation-effect will get most girls through the pain-barrier, though if you make her bleed at all give time for abrasions to heal before the next round. If it's more troublesome than this, get advice (see *Defloration*). With gentleness and preliminary stretching it can be quite painless in most women.

Actual craving for pain (mental or physical) as a sex kick isn't uncommon. Usually the idea is exciting in fantasy but a turn-off in practice, unless your partner is skilled enough to keep inside the limits of transformation by excitement, and the fantasy itself isn't too violent. A good many men who have persuaded a not over-intelligent whore to 'beat them hard' because the idea sounded exciting have been choked off a repeat performance. If your partner has such fantasies, keep well inside their powers of stimulus-transformation, subtract a good twenty percent from the fantasy, and watch out for the occasional sick character who really enjoys the idea of being injured. For sane people commonsense, a bit of play-acting, and intelligent use of the transformation effect can more than take care of the normal fantasy-range.

perversion

In books prior to the seventies, this meant, quite simply, any sexual behavior which the writer didn't himself enjoy. More correctly, it means something antisocial which handicapped people use as a substitute for the sexuality from which their hangups debar them. The commonest perversions in our culture are getting hold of some power and using it to kick other people around, money-hunting as a status activity, treating other people, sexually or otherwise, as things to manipulate, and interfering with other people's sex lives to ensure that they are as rigid and as anxious about them as the interferer. Scheduled perversions like digging up corpses or committing lust murder are confined almost wholly to borderline psychotics, and, though obviously serious, are of less social importance than the respectable kinds because they are rare and disapproved of. It's a measure of the prestige of socially approved perversion that most public utterances in legislation, law enforcement and so on genuflect to what are basically perverse attitudes, even when the speakers are privately healthy and don't live by what they say.

Hangups of this sort are extremely difficult to cure, whether they lead to sadistic mutilation, purity crusading, Belsen or Vietnam. However sorry you are for the possessors, they are dangerous people and best avoided as partners or as mentors – you will only be asking for a lot of trouble.

priapism

From Priapus, the Roman garden god with a large stiff wooden penis: erection you don't want and can't get rid of, unaccompanied by any feeling of sexual pleasure or excitement at all.

A painful erection which won't go away is rare, and a sign as a rule of something wrong, and you should see a doctor. What is commoner, though not common, is being woken at night by painful, non-pleasant erections, even when one has had a full ejaculation, so that the patient has to get up and walk around or shower – intercourse or masturbation does not help: the result can be severe loss of sleep. Mentioned here because the sufferers worry themselves gray about it. The cause isn't known – it may be psychological (it often stops away from home). All normal males get repeated erections in sleep, but usually these don't wake them or are accompanied by pleasantly sexy feelings, not pain. There doesn't seem to be a good remedy for this trouble. Drugs which turn it off are apt to turn off potency. Fortunately the symptom usually goes away, and whatever treatment you were having at the time gets the credit. Does not interfere with sex at other times.

prostitution

Prostitutes don't as a rule either practice or enjoy advanced lovemaking. This isn't true in all cultures, but in ours the commonest motive for becoming a regular streetwalking pro is an active dislike of males. Their attraction insofar as it persists is in part mythological, and also due to their un-shocked understanding of unscheduled sex needs, the fact that the man can at least be sure of getting sex from them without social hangups, and a group of feelings connected with sharing a woman with other males. No doubt if we treated the professional as other cultures have done – on all fours with the concert artist who gives up domesticity to an art – the personnel of professional sex would improve and it would lose its present psycho-pathology, and be of help both to bothered clients and the girls themselves, but general sexual freedom is more likely to displace monetary sex altogether, except for those for whom it arises from unconscious needs.

Apart from the attractions we've mentioned, any woman who herself is ready to enjoy and understand sex, and meet her partner's needs as fully as a professional but with love, can outclass anyone hired. She can learn from periods and cultures in which the courtesan was a repository of the art of pleasing, but what we call whores' tricks ought to be called lovers' tricks. A woman who can make love with love and variety needn't fear commercial competition.

If your man goes to a prostitute, it's either because he was away from you, or because he has sex needs you didn't know about, or because of the shared-woman no-responsibility bit (which in the most loving males can still be very strong), or simply because of impulse which he doesn't understand. Even if you are hurt about it, try to find out the reason, because knowing it could help a lot.

rape

Lovers will play rape *games* without end, but the real thing is a frightening turn-off. It may sound unpleasant, but is worth knowing, that the surefire way a woman can resist rape, armed or not, is by suddenly emptying her bowels. Few rapists will persist after that, and it doesn't involve provocative and maybe ineffectual physical assault.

Don't get yourself raped – i.e. don't deliberately excite a man you don't know well, unless you mean to follow through.

smoking

Heavy cigarette smoking considerably shortens life. It can also interfere quite considerably with potency, and can make mouth-to-mouth kissing unpleasant, or at least unrewarding. At the same time the odor of pipe or cigar tobacco registers with some women as part of maleness:

others dislike it. Why we enjoy inhaling smoke isn't biologically obvious – nicotine has some drug action, but quite a few mammals and birds are 'turned on' by smoke. Crows even pick up lighted cigarette butts and pass them over their feathers, while fire, with attendant smoke, was a prehuman social discovery. Sucking, of course, is a universal and lifelong turn-on for man. There's also a whole anthropology of who smokes what connected with sex roles – pipes for women have never caught on fully in our culture.

Luckily, we don't need to spell all this out in order to take a line through it. Cigarettes are better avoided by lovers as by gourmets, both from the danger angle and the slob effect of bad breath and dirty hands: pipes and cigars less so. A lot of nicotine can, in some people, interfere physically with erection. If you aim to stop smoking, do it totally, but make your resolution a day at a time, and use sex as a displacement activity while you are getting over the gap. It's more effective than overeating and better for you.

Pot has complex pharmacological actions, but in our society it acts chiefly as a social irritant, producing a feeling of agreeable defiance in users and a suspension of rational thought in non-users. Its dangers have been deliberately exaggerated as a result of this effect. Doctors who already have to deal with alcohol, pills, aspirin and the like reckon that we need more pharmacological kicks like we need a hole in the head, but there are two views on this. One thing it isn't is an aphrodisiac. Most lovers who really enjoy sex prefer to start straight and let the things they do give them a high – which is what short-cut kicks are a substitute for.

termination

In a well-conducted sex life it shouldn't be necessary. All ethics apart, neither you nor the doctor can be quite sure how a woman – or a couple – will react to it psychologically. The present boom is due less to permissive legislation than to the fact that women who have been scared off the Pill by deliberate alarmism, but have experienced the effects of really reliable troublefree birth control, are simply not willing either to go back to the old makeshifts or to have unwanted children.

At the factual level, early abortion (in the first 3 months) done by a qualified expert in a properly equipped hospital is, physically, a minor and safe operation. Done by an unqualified person, a backroom consultant, or a do-it-yourself method it is dangerous and psychologically searing. Done too late (and some physicians who object to all abortion on principle deliberately try to delay matters until it is too late, and then tell you so with a superior grin) it involves killing a potentially viable child.

If you plan your sex life properly and take informed and conscientious contraceptive precautions, you shouldn't need to terminate a pregnancy except on exceptional grounds. Odd that the main moral woe-criers on abortion are also the people who have done most to block proper birth control and starve research and education about it of funds.

transvetitism

Many people enjoy dressing in each other's clothes on occasion for the hell of it. That isn't transvestitism. A transvestite is a person who, while staying fully in his or her own sex role, feels an intense compulsion at times to dress the opposite sex role, and an intense release of anxiety (not so much a kick) when they do so. They are not 'homosexual,' and a bisexual person who dresses the opposite sex to please a partner isn't a transvestite. A transexualist is a person, usually male, who actively wants to turn into a person of the other sex, by surgery if necessary, and feels totally miscast as they are. In some simpler societies there are roles or ceremonies which discharge these needs (wizards often cross-dress). In our society they can cause intense anxiety. A transvestite with an informed and unscared wife usually finds that his compulsion, whatever its cause, doesn't spoil his sex-life in the male role (if he has to keep it secret or she thinks he's queer or crazy, which he isn't, he can get really sick from worry); a transexualist needs expert help and may or may not be the happier for a sex-change operation. A lot of unhappiness could be avoided if people knew the facts to the point of not being scared or shocked if they come across them. If you have a partner with any of these problems, help them by comprehension and see they get help from an expert.

vasectomy

This is the one reliable, once-and-for-all male contraceptive method. It consists of closing off, by a small surgical operation, the tubes down which the sperms travel from the testis. The operation is done under local anesthetic. It hurts rather less than having a small cut stitched, and you can go straight home. The long-term result is a completely virile but infertile male. (Repeat, competent vasectomy carries absolutely no risk of physical interference with, erection, ejaculation, sexual feelings, or virility generally – under the name of 'Steinach's operation' it used to be done as a rejuvenation treatment and virility booster.) If you have all the children you-want (which, if you have a sense of responsibility, shouldn't in most cases be more than two) consider it seriously. Certainly consider it rather than making your woman undergo the much bigger operation needed to sterilize her, or keeping her on the Pill if it doesn't suit her.

There are a few more factual points to consider.

1 Vasectomy doesn't make you sterile at once. Sperms can hang around for months, so you must stick to your previous birth control method until you know you are clear. After that you can both forget about birth control.

2 You can't change your mind. Vasectomy is sometimes reversible, but you mustn't count on that. It's a calculated risk that you might suddenly want to father children later, but not worth hanging back for if otherwise it looks right for you. No decision one takes is one hundred percent safe, but if you wanted more children there are unwanted babies wanting adoption, assuming you are fit people.

3 On the other hand, make sure you know your own feelings – which in any matter connected with sex and reproduction are never wholly reasonable. If the doctor refuses to do the operation 'off the shelf' without discussing your general self-picture of maleness, that only shows that he knows his job. If he refuses on principle or because he doesn't like your life style, consult another doctor.

If you are married, have had two wanted children or don't want children, and have any contraceptive problems, give vasectomy serious thought. If you're spread wider than that and have any sense of responsibility, you should be vasectomized. You can buy a 'vasectomy tie' or pin to advertise the fact. Wearing one when you haven't been operated is a cad's trick – far more so than wearing Guards or Ivy League colors you aren't entitled to. In case of argument, the girl can check the two little scars.

It may be possible eventually to store some of your sperm in the deep-freeze as an insurance, but you won't be able to do this now.

venereal diseases

These have been covertly fostered for several generations by straight Society as God's punishment for sin. On the other hand, they are a real hazard of having intercourse, or heavy petting, with people you don't know. There are two common ones. Syphilis is a killing disease – the first sign is a relatively painless sore where you have been infected (genitals, anus, mouth) followed some time later by a generalized rash, and years later by a great many unpleasant sequels. It can even be transmitted from mother to unborn baby. Gonorrhea ('clap') usually shows up in the male within a week as a painful discharge from the penis. In the woman it can cause discharge and swollen glands, but may be symptomless and far more easily missed. Both are no trouble to treat if you go at once. *Don't* try to treat them yourselves with antibiotics and whatever the repercussions don't try to cover up, but warn anyone you may have infected. In fact, if it weren' for the aura of magic, either one would be a far preferable choice to having measles. There is another less common 'venereal' disease (lymphogranuloma inguinale), and you can catch crab lice from a dirty partner. People who sleep around, and some who don't, can catch and transmit trichomoniasis — don't assume infidelity if your partner gets this, but both of you, and any third parties, will need treatment to get rid of it.

If you must take risks, washing thoroughly with soap and passing water immediately after intercourse are a fair protection — so is wearing a condom, but remember that syphilis can be spread by kissing. Don't have intercourse with anyone who has a discharge or sores. But one mega-unit or oral penicillin taken within 1–2 hours of contact is practically 100 percent protection, even now, when some germs are relatively resistant. If you know you are taking risks you could take the dose beforehand ('St. Peter's Umbrella' — after the apostle who toiled all night and caught nothing). The moralists are quite right in saying that avoiding partners who are easy is the best prophylactic, but even that isn't 100 percent.

Venereal diseases could be stamped out altogether in our generation if people stopped treating them as a special case, and if nobody had a vested interest in them as a deterrent. Prostitutes aren't the chief source of infection — the big risks are careless and ignorant amateurs. Homosexuals can and do catch them as well as heterosexuals, in fact more frequently. Being on the Pill greatly increases the risk for a woman — not because it affects her morals, but because it knocks out a natural antiseptic mechanism.

Some of your best friends quite likely have V.D.

waterworks

Children are fascinated by watching one another urinate. So are some adults. There is no special reason to be ashamed of this; it's another childhood game, simply.

A few women are embarrassed that intense sex excitement makes them 'spend a penny' involuntarily. This occurs in animals too and can be avoided by emptying the bladder beforehand. Very violent sex for a very long time can bruise the female bladder and produce a good imitation of an attack of cystitis ('honeymoon bladder'). This soon clears with a few days' rest—avoid any positions which set it off. Women liable to repeated attacks of cystitis can sometimes avoid trouble by passing water immediately after intercourse.

Most males get a stronger erection, and feel more, on a full bladder, but may find some positions painful if it's very full. We never heard of a bladder being ruptured, but older men with prostate trouble might do well not to cultivate the technique. Normally, a male can't urinate with an erection: there is a two-way valve built into the system. In women the mouth of the urethra is nearly as sensitive as the clitoris, but it is a bad idea to put tapers or hairpins into it by way of masturbation – doctors often have to remove these from the bladder.

Index